SHAWNEE

**DO NOT REMOVE
CARDS FROM POCKET**

Arnie &
a House Full of Company

Also available in Large Print
by Margarete Sigl Corbo and Diane Marie Barras:

Arnie, the Darling Starling

Arnie
&

a House Full of Company

Margarete Sigl Corbo
and Diane Marie Barras

Illustrated by Ryan Stuart Young

G.K.HALL &CO.
Boston, Massachusetts
1986

Copyright © 1985 by Margarete Sigl Corbo and
Diane Marie Barras.

All rights reserved.

Published in Large Print by arrangement
with Houghton Mifflin Company.

G. K. Hall Large Print Book Series.

Set in 16 pt Plantin.

Library of Congress Cataloging in Publication Data

Corbo, Margarete Sigl.
  Arnie & a house full of company.

  (G.K. Hall large print book series)
  Sequel to: Arnie, the darling starling.
  1. Starlings as pets.   2. Starlings—Biography.
3. Corbo, Margarete Sigl.   4. Large type books.
I. Barras, Diane Marie.   II. Title.   III. Title:
Arnie and a house full of company.
[SF473.S9C65   1986]   818'.5403   86-14996
ISBN 0-8161-4077-4 (lg. print)

Warning. *This story is rated "G" for all ages, but it is intended for the warm of heart only. Readers may find it a special sharing experience. Tongue-in-cheek discretion is advised; the rigidly scientific of mind may regard the material as offensive (forgive them, for they know not what joys they miss). It is a completely true tale, though the authors have used considerable literary license. The names of some of the human characters have been changed, but the entire cast of Arnie's Company is as real as your own family and friends.*

For our families,
especially the roots:

Johann & Katherina Sigl
Vincent & Marie Barras
Raymond & Bertie Carter

You can never go back, or so they say,

To home, to life, to loves of yesterday.
It's true, of course; but, thinking another way,

Today's foundation was built upon that
    yesterday

While tomorrow's promise is only a dream
    away.
Grab each while you can; hold tight while you
    may.
Your future depends upon what you do with this
    day,

And a bright tomorrow takes a clear eye on
    yesterday.

1 Singing at the top of my lungs, I swung the Blazer into the driveway, slammed on the brakes, and gasped. "Where's the house? Somebody's stolen my house!"

Aghast, I tumbled from the car and looked around. The modest Cape Cod ranch in which my family had lived for more than twenty years was nowhere in sight. The quarter-acre lot upon which it should be so clearly evident was a dense miniforest surrounded by a thicket of tall hedges. And amidst it all stood I—cold, tired, hungry, bewildered, and trapped by that behemoth of a trailer I'd just hauled two thousand miles from Texas.

I leaned my head back, closed my eyes, and

shouted with frustration. "Is there an idle jinni around? My three wishes are simple: a hot shower, a crackling fire, and a bowl of steaming clam chowder!"

It was one of those raw days that invariably chase away the last remnants of tourists and summer residents, relegating Cape Cod to the small permanent population quirky enough to thrive on its off-season isolation. My Windbreaker flapped with loud cracks, assaulted by chill gusts announcing that winter was only one good nor'easter away. Tendrils of mist, pushing in from Vineyard Sound, eddied and swirled like ghostly dancers in the fading, gray daylight. The normal brilliance of autumn's colorful tapestry was subdued, somber. Aside from the wind and the occasional lowing of a distant foghorn, there were no sounds about me, no signs of activity to lessen the desolation I felt.

Taking a few steps to the side, I searched for the sidewalk that had to be somewhere beneath the sweeping spruce branches. A flurry of mourning doves rose from the ground, startling me with their labored wing beats and soft cries of distress. Tracking their flight, I spotted the silvery sheen of well-weathered cedar shingles peeping through evergreen needles. A drainpipe, torn loose from the gutter, caught my eye as it wobbled stiffly within the loosening grasp of a metal strap binding it. Nature had stolen my house from view and begun to ravage it, but it was in there, within the trees, waiting for me to reclaim it.

I sighed, opened the back of the Blazer, and rummaged among the tools until I found the one I needed.

"Happy homecoming," I grumbled. "Maybe coming back wasn't such a smart move after all." I swung the ax over my shoulder and down. Wood splintered, satisfyingly. I pushed up my sleeves and swung the ax again and again. Each destructive blow eased my pain a bit, but the hollow sensation around my heart was still there when I rested the ax against the house.

Stepping onto the stoop, I fished in my pocket, found the key my brother had mailed to me, and slipped it into the doorknob. The lock clicked quietly, and the door opened a tiny crack. I drew in a deep, ragged breath, held it a long moment, let it out slowly, and gave the door a push. Silently, it glided halfway open, then bumped to a stop against a bulging black plastic garbage bag in the entry hall. I stepped in. A spider web engulfed the right side of my face, clinging to my nose and eye with the intimacy of a second skin. Rubbing frantically at it, I leaped backward and teetered on the edge of the stoop.

"No way will I go inside alone," I muttered. I started to walk, then broke into a trot, not slowing until I reached the car. Glancing over my shoulder, I could see one window, its shutters askew and broken. Through the window shone a light I hadn't noticed before. Yet the house had been unoccupied for years, and I possessed its only keys. Jittery with wild imaginings about what the light might signify, I yanked open the car door and was barraged by a cacophony of mournful yowls.

"Keep your complaints to yourselves, cats," I said. "My nerves can't take your nonsense today." Reaching into the back seat, I wrestled out two of the travel cages, rushed with them to the house, and shoved them inside the door. "Yell all you want now," I said. "In fact, please do yell. Growl! Hiss a little, even. Sound ferocious! If there's an intruder here, let him know I'm not alone." My black-furred felines stared at me—silently. "I'm going to trade you two in for a Doberman yet," I said as I turned for another trip to the car.

The screech of thin-shoed brakes shattered the silence. I arrived at the driveway in time to see the hood of a faded orange Volkswagen sliding neatly beneath the rear end of the rental trailer hitched to my car. The woman behind the wheel of the VW had her eyes tightly closed. Any moment would come the sound of the impact, the scrunching of crushing metal, the tinkling of shattering glass, the human scream. Cravenly, I turned my back, ducked my head, and covered my ears with my hands. I head a thud, then—

"Maa-gret, Maa-gret," called a voice with a hearty Boston accent. "It's really you! I couldn't believe it when I heard your voice on the phone."

"You didn't have to rush over so fast, M.A.," I said, looking up with relief. The windshield of the VW was only a few inches short of impact, a fact of which the driver appeared oblivious as she strode toward me with a welcoming smile.

Mary Alice hadn't changed a bit in the twenty

4

years since my daughter had introduced us. She would tell no one her age, though I was certain she was older than Hannelore and younger than I. Her long, strong-featured face was framed by light auburn hair that spilled over her wool plaid poncho and brushed past the Levi's label on the pocket of her jeans. Her every gesture was flamboyant and, apparently, she still drove with complete abandon.

"You almost turned your car into a convertible this time, didn't you?" I knew what her response would be, of course; my little scoldings and her little defenses were ritual between us, as though I were a second mother and she another daughter.

"Now, Maa-gret, you know I'm a good driver. I do need to get those brakes fixed, though. Oh, poor Christmas trees. Look how you've butchered them!"

"I had no choice. Seems that Hanna and I planted them too close to the house. The lower branches had to go so I could get to the front door. Looks like the place has reverted to jungle."

She looked around, tsk–tsking in sympathy at the dilapidated condition of the house and yard. "Don't worry," she said, "you'll have it shaped up in no time."

"I'm not so sure I'll bother. I thought I was finally ready to come back, but now that I'm here . . . ." I shrugged. "I don't know if I'll be able to stay. I feel like a displaced person."

"You're tired, that's all," she said.

"And cranky. And cold. Let's get into the house. Here, don't go empty-handed" I thrust a paper bag and the litter box at M.A., then led the way, carrying the third cat and the birdcage. As I paused in the doorway, working up my courage to take the big step inside, she spoke in a normal voice that jarred me as too-loud for the moment, saying, "I see you still have the bird and the cat."

"Same cat, plus two others–different bird." I whispered as I took one cautious step, then another, through the door. The lamp beside my mother's chair was on, as was the light in the kitchen that had always been her domain. I expected at any moment to see Mama walking around the breakfast bar, drying her hands on her apron, squinting as she struggled with almost-blind eyes to see me. I took another step and felt the warmth of the house embracing me, the nurturing warmth of home. It was as if I had just been down the road to the grocery store, instead of absent for seven years, as if the life and love and laughter of the entire family were still housed within these four walls.

"Why are you whispering?" M.A. asked.

"I don't know," I said aloud. "It's so strange having this house empty. I wrote ahead to have the electricity turned on, but it was eerie to see lights shining through the window. Guess my brother forgot to turn them off when he locked up." I put the birdcage on the coffee table and whisked off its cover, then opened the doors that confined the cats. Cautiously, they stepped out into the room and began a sniffing exploration of the new surroundings that would undoubtedly keep them busy for hours.

"Let's put the litter box in the bathroom," I said,

peeking around the corner into the empty kitchen. It was a chore I could have done myself, but deep in my timorous heart I wanted an escort while I ensured the security of the house. Close on my heels, M.A. kept up a running chatter as I flipped on lights and inspected the other rooms. Though the beds were neatly made, vacant closets gaped open and crooked drawers gave evidence of a hasty emptying in the two bedrooms where my parents had spent their last days. In each, fallen tree branches protruded through broken windows and icy wind gusted in, making the rooms downright frigid. Glad for the excuse, I closed the doors behind us; tomorrow was soon enough to cope with the realities of those unoccupied rooms.

"Help me settle in for the night, will you? There are a few things I need, but I don't have the energy to struggle with that trailer again today."

"Why don't you sleep at my house and start fresh in the morning?"

"Thank you, but no."

Clutching my hastily scribbled list, M.A. backed the VW out of the drive, waving as she drove off. I grabbed a suitcase and the overnight bag from the car. Something brushed my ankle, scurried past, and stopped a few steps down the walkway. Looking up at me, a gray squirrel with white belly fur stood tall on its hind legs, its eyes brightly curious, its nose twitching, its front paws held out as though begging alms. "Well, hello," I said. "Guess you and I are going to be neighbors." It cocked its head to one side, gave me three brisk tail waggles, and bounced away to join two other squirrels atop the pile of spruce branches. Like an audience, they watched as I struggled with my burden up the steps and through the door, then tripped over the garbage bag blocking the way. Muttering, I picked myself up off the floor and grabbed at the cause of my mishap. A jumble of undergarments spilled out of the bag onto the floor. Soiled with emptied cigarette ashes, neatly folded slips and gowns lay among entwined stockings and socks, cotton panties, and lacy handkerchiefs. Numbly, I stared.

"Is that you, Mrs. Corbo? Margarete? Are you all right? You're pale as a ghost!"

"Huh? Yes, I'm fine," I said. Stuffing my mother's intimate apparel back into the garbage bag, I smiled at the middle-aged blond woman standing in the doorway. "How are you, April?"

"Welcome home, my dear. Welcome home," she said and stepped forward to hug me. "I saw the trailer when I got home from work and rushed right over, hoping it was you. I was beginning to fear you might never come back. Oh, it's so *good* to see you!"

"Hi there," Arnie said from his cage. "Hi there. C'mere. Gimme a kiss."

"Oh!" April said. "He startled me. I had forgotten about your parrot. He talks so clearly now!"

"The parrot died years ago, I'm afraid. Arnie's just a common wild bird."

"But . . . but, didn't I just hear him talk?" She walked over and looked into the cage. "Peek-a-boo. How are you?" Arnie said. April put her hand over her open mouth and leaned closer to the cage.

8

"You're no more astonished than I was when he first talked," I said. "He was just an ordinary wild baby when I found him. He'd fallen from his nest into my daisies—didn't even have a feather on his body. I was certain he would die, but I brought him into the house and fed him, and, well, before I knew what was happening, he'd twisted me right around his little talon. I've been his faithful servant ever since."

"I love you, yes I do," Arnie said. "C'mere, kiss Arnie. He's a little bitty baby boy, yes he is."

"He's adorable!" April said. "I can't wait to tell Ricky and Nancy. Speaking of which, I'd better get dinner on the table for those kids of mine. Remember, my dear, if there's anything you need, we're right next door."

As she disappeared through the hedges between our houses, I realized I was still clutching the plastic garbage bag. "Oh, Mama . . . Papa . . . You're really gone, aren't you?" I wailed into the silence. "Hanna's grown and on her own. And it's a cinch that Frank and I will never patch up our marriage. It's painful being here with all the reminders of the way things were. I feel as lost and lonely as I did when I landed in New York as a young immigrant. What am I going to do with the rest of my life?"

The Volkswagen screeched to a halt outside. "I'm going to quit feeling sorry for myself for starters," I mumbled as I tied a knot into the neck of the garbage bag. "I have faithful friends and nice neighbors and my animal companions, and I'm going to spend the winter here if it kills me, that's what I'm

9

going to do!" I asserted as I tossed the bag down the basement stairs. "And I'm going to quit talking to myself before someone overhears and has me committed."

"It's going to freeze tonight," M.A. said as she banged through the door, laden with groceries and an electric heater. "You won't have heat until your water's turned on, so I thought this would come in handy. I threw a load of wood into the car, too. We can get the fireplace going, drag a mattress out here in front of it, and you should be snug for the night, Maa-gret."

I put on a pot of coffee while she introduced herself to the animals. "Ahhhh, what a darlin'," I heard her saying as I poured water from a bottle into the electric coffee maker. When I looked around the corner, Arnie was watching her as intently as she was him. She moved to one side of the cage to see him better, and he scooted along his perch to be near her. "I've never seen a bird like him before," she said over her shoulder. "Does he sing?"

"You've probably seen more birds like Arnie than any other kind you can imagine," I said. "You've just never seen one in a cage before. He's a starling."

"Really? You mean those pesky things that are always pecking around in the yard? Why, I spend half my summers chasing them out of my garden. He can't be one of them, though. They're black and homely. Arnie has brown and white specks, and he's so cute!"

"The others have the specks, too. You've just

10

never really paid attention to starlings. No one ever does because they're so commonplace."

"If they're so commonplace, whey are you bothering with this one?"

"Arnie's special, M.A.; very special. Sit down and drink your coffee. I have a long, very interesting story to tell you about that common little wild bird."

She was on her third cup of coffee when I finished telling her an elaborate version of the same tale I'd told April. She'd interrupted with questions and laughter while I talked, but now she was silent. Looking intently at Arnie in his cage, she reached down to scratch one of the cats. Removing the cigarette from her mouth, she appeared about to speak, changed her mind, and inhaled another drag of smoke. Slowly, she began to shake her head from side to side, did a prolonged tsk-tsk-tsk with her tongue, then started to laugh.

"You almost had me that time, Maa-gret. I almost believed you. Only you could get away with convincing me that you'd taught a wild bird to talk. I've been sitting here listening for him to say something, then I realized you were pulling my leg."

"I am not pulling your leg, M.A., really I'm not. Say something, Arnie. Oh, never mind. I know from experience that he won't utter a sound right now. He seems to know exactly when his silence will make me look like a complete fool. Just you wait, though. When you're least expecting it, he'll talk."

"Well," she said, smiling broadly and punctuating every other word with quick jabs of her cigarette into the air, "this will certainly be a tale to tell Mother. She's always said I bring back more interesting stories from your house than she sees on television."

"How is Marie?"

M.A.'s mother was a slight, pretty woman with flawless, alabaster skin, a quick wit, and a brilliant mind. Unfortunately, her body was her worst enemy. When I'd met her, Marie was already bent almost double by a particularly nasty form of arthritis. Though M.A. had been an industrious, ambitious young woman, she hadn't been able to hold a regular job in years because she was the only thing standing between her mother and a rest home. At my question, M.A. shrugged, and a cloud flickered over her eyes. "She's bedridden most of the time now. But her mind is bright as ever." She smiled. "She'll probably keep me up all night asking questions about your travels."

"Go home and start talking, then," I said. "Thanks for coming over. I really needed a friend today."

"Are you certain you don't want to come home with me? I don't think I could stay here if I were you."

"Don't be silly. I've roughed it much more than I'll be doing tonight."

"That's not what I mean. Aren't you afraid?"

"Afraid? Why on earth would I be afraid?"

"Well . . ." She hesitated, glanced over her shoulder, and lowered her voice. "Your father died right here in the house, didn't he? Maybe his spirit is still here."

I laughed. "M.A., I don't believe in ghosts. Besides, even if I did, I would never worry about my father haunting me. We had a very good relationship."

She laughed, too, but nervously. "You're right, of course. Still, it's almost Halloween. If there are spirits, this is the time of year they're supposed to be restless and roaming, you know."

I shrugged off her words as nonsense, but they came vividly to mind some hours later, when I was jarred from a sound sleep by noises in the night.

Ka-thump! Flutter, flutter, flutter. *Thud!* Flap, flutter, flap. Thump. Thud! Ka-thump!! *Flutter, flap, flap, flutter.* Thump-thud!!

"Mmmph! What's that?" I sat upright and stared into the darkness. Stretched out on his back, his head resting on the pillow next to mine, my husky male cat slept much like a little human boy. Bundy's gentle snores and an occasional crackle in the fireplace were the only sounds I could hear now. I listened intently for a while, then shrugged. "Must have been a dream," I muttered and lay back down. "Just a dream, thank goodness."

Flap, flap, flutter, flutter, flutter. Ka-thud! Thump-thud-thunk. Flap, flap. *Kwomp!* Flutter, flutter, flutter, flutter, flutter.

So much for wishful thinking. The noises were real, not part of a dream after all. That was Arnie flying around in his cage, bumping about in the dark. I jumped to my feet.

13

"Calm down, Arnie," I said, bending over to look into his cage. "What's the problem?"

There was just enough moonlight filtering into the room to allow me to make out his shadowy form clinging to the front door screening. His neck was stretched to its utmost extreme. Rapid, loud panting sounds told me of his extreme fright. Something tickled my leg just as he leaped toward his top perch, overshot the mark, and fell to the floor of the cage.

"Maaaaaoooww," Samantha said in the shrill voice she's inherited from a mere few drops of Siamese blood. She rubbed her nose against my leg again, then stood up to look into Arnie's cage.

He cowered in a corner, not so much as twitching a feather. "I'm just a big, terrifying blob in the dark to you, huh?" I said. "No wonder you're afraid." I switched on a lamp. "There, that's better, isn't it?" Uttering agitated little trrrpppping sounds, Arnie ran to the cage door and frantically pried at it with his mandibles. I sighed. "Well, I'm up for the night, anyway. You might as well join me." I opened the cage door and reached down so he could hop onto my hand. With a brief flutter of wings, he moved from there to my shoulder, softly whistled the first eight notes of Beethoven's Fifth Symphony into my ear, and snuggled against my neck.

Samantha crept to the fireplace, crouched, and peered around the corner and down the hallway. Her tail whipped from side to side. She stared at me for a moment, then glared at the mirror on my father's bedroom door, and hissed. "Only silly cats

14

hiss at themselves, Sammie," I said. "There's nothing there but your own reflection." Deep in her throat, she began to growl. "C'mon, see for yourself," I said.

With a ferocious feline at my feet and a savage starling on my shoulder, I was inspired to act more bravely than I felt as I opened the doors and peeked into the bedrooms. Curtains flapped in the north wind gusting through the broken windows. Outside, something banged loudly against the side of the house. My heart skipped a beat, jumped into my throat, and started keeping time to the *William Tell* Overture. Samantha made a sudden spurting run past me and down the hallway. "What are you doing?" Arnie demanded. I slammed the bedroom door shut and checked the thick stick wedged beneath the knob of the basement door. In the living room, Sammie scuttled from one window to another, crouching below the sills as she peeked out. "Brraddddtttt! You go to sleep. You go to sleep!" Arnie scolded as she ran up to me, skidded through a U-turn, and pounced back to a window.

Resisting the temptation to crouch below the sill myself, I stood behind Sammie and strained to see what was upsetting her so. Shadows moved in the yard. With trembling hands, I switched on the outside lights and looked again. Tree branches and bushes bent and bobbed, buffeted by the wind, but nothing else was there. "You have a very vivid imagination, Sammie," I said with relief. "If something was really lurking about, Mitzi and Bundy would have been in on the action, but neither of them has moved a muscle—thank goodness."

I gave the coals in the fireplace a stir and threw on a few sticks of wood. Reassuring myself with a final glance out the windows, I lit a cigarette, turned off the lamp, and settled into an easy chair to let my nerves calm. "If I'm jittery, it's partly M.A.'s fault, Arnie," I said. "Her parting words sounded like some of Mama's superstitious nonsense. Ghosts and goblins, vampires and curses . . . I think my mother believed in them all. Not me, though. Uh-uh. Not me."

Something bumped beyond the end of the hallway.

"Good morning!" Arnie rasped. "Good morning."

Mitzi and Bundy snapped awake.

Behind my father's bedroom door, a floorboard squeaked, sounding for all the world as though someone had stepped on it. Side by side, the three cats crouched, tails swishing in unison, their widened eyes fixed on that door. Arnie pressed so tightly against my neck that he could have been mistaken for a surgical implant.

"It's just the wind." I soothed them. "Remember, the windows are broken in those rooms. There is nothing for us to be afraid of."

Then why is the hair rising on the nape of my neck? I wondered.

"It's just an automatic reaction to seeing the fur rise on the backs of the three cats," I answered myself.

I gulped, suddenly feeling very cold. My hands

17

were so clammy I doubted if I'd be able to grip the lamp for which I was groping on the panicky notion that I needed a weapon.

"*If there are spirts, this is the time of year they're supposed to be restless and roaming . . .*" M.A. had said.

I was in midstep when the sound of a loud crash froze me into immobility. My heart beat so furiously it felt as though it would burst out of my chest.

The crash had come from the bedroom in which my father had slept—and died.

2 To grow older is to acquire an ever stronger sense of mortality; and as the accompanying realization of personal frailty dawns, acts once admired as brave begin to seem merely foolish. Thus it is that some of us manage to survive to a ripe old age: we get smart enough to become cowardly.

Cats, apparently, are genetically endowed with that bit of wisdom—at least my three cats are. At the sound of the crash, Mitzi spurted to a far corner and crouched, ready to defend herself it necessary, but unwilling to go looking for trouble. Vagabond, for whom the term *scaredy-cat* was invented, hugged the ground so tightly as he ran that he looked like a bug scurrying for cover. Sammie nudged him to

greater speed and, together, they disappeared beneath a chair. Proving that birds are no dummies,
either, Arnie took to the heights and claimed the
safety of a curtain rod.

Unfortunately, I hadn't lived long enough to acquire my full share of wisdom. Curiosity compelled
me to check out the bedroom, to find out what had
caused the noises that upset us all. And common
sense told me to do it without hesitation, lest I have
too much time to contemplate the possibilities.

Step by careful, quiet step, I crept down the hallway toward my father's old bedroom. Memories of
Papa, more haunting than any spirit could have
been, were conjured up by that closed door. It had
always signaled that he was sulking his way through
a family squabble; when it remained that way for
long, when he began to drop things so that thumps
and bumps began to emerge from behind it, we'd
known that his pride needed salvaging, that it was
time for someone to peep inside the room and cajole
him to rejoin the family. Given free rein, my imagination would easily indulge the part of my heart
that wanted to believe he really was in there now,
waiting to greet me with a smile and teasing words
about how the women in his life never allowed a
man a moment's privacy. I could almost smell his
cigar smoke, almost hear a snatch of country music
drifting from his radio, almost believe the crash I'd
heard was one of his typical peace gestures.

The broken window provided a likely explanation for the noise, however—there was an intruder
in the house. How simple for someone to reach

20

through that hole in the glass, quietly turn the lock and lift the window, then climb surreptitiously through the opening. There might be a raving lunatic on the other side of that door, or maybe a notorious cat burglar! Well, whoever it was was wasting his time: there were no family jewels here, and most of the household silver was monogrammed "stainless steel."

As I reached for the doorknob with my left hand, I hefted the lamp in my right. It had a good, solid feel to it, a comforting feel. I was as prepared as I was ever going to be for the situation.

Slowly, ever so quietly, I turned the knob.

Centimeter by centimeter, I eased the door open, leaned forward, put my eye to the widening crack, and peered into the room. It was pitch black. I could see nothing. But was that someone breathing in there? With a measured quietness intended to avoid detection? And that dark blob over in the far corner—was that someone crouching behind the bed?

Suddenly it dawned on me that the light from the room behind me must be shining as brightly as a floodlamp through that tiny crack in the door. If I was having trouble seeing the intruder, he was certainly having no trouble seeing me. To even the odds, I flipped the wall switch; the room was bathed in brightness.

The covers on the bed were in disarray. A lamp lay on the floor. My father's radio, to which I'd listened while getting settled for the night, had been moved from the spot where I'd left it.

Otherwise, the room was empty.

I would have shrugged, rationalized an explanation for the covers and the lamp, chalked off the squeaking floorboard to an overactive imagination, discounted the entire scare, if not for one fact of which I was certain: I remembered vividly exactly where I had put that radio. It had been moved only a foot or so, but that foot or so had it placed right back on the exact same spot it had always occupied when Papa was alive.

The old, rigid household rule popped into my mind: *It's verboten to touch anything in Papa's room.*

"Well, it's not his room anymore," I said to M.A. over coffee the next day. "Besides, that's not the explanation. Papa would never . . . I mean . . . oh, you know what I mean."

It still hurt to think about him. In one part of my mind, I suppose I'd thought him indestructible. There was an entire family history of reasons for that irrational sentiment, of course: like the time, during the World War II bombardment of our home in Munich, when a bomb had crashed through the wall of my bedroom and lodged there unexploded, but likely to go off at any time. We'd been in a bomb shelter when it fell, but for the inhabitants of our apartment building, danger waited for us to be lulled into a sense of security.

I wouldn't have found the bomb in time, either, if not for Medie, my parakeet, who teased me into a game of chase that led me to the bedroom. When I ran through the door looking for her, I was laugh-

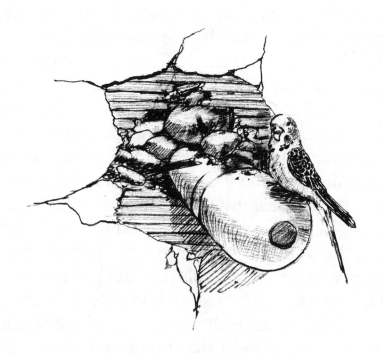

ing with the fun of the game. Medie was sitting about three feet above the head of my bed. watching for me to come through the door after her. The object upon which she perched was the protruding tip of the bomb. Medie flapped her wings vigorously, hopped up and down and around in circles, and chirped unceasingly. Maybe that was just part of the game to her, but I'd played many games with Medie over the years, and she'd never acted that way before.

I knew more about bombs then than any child anywhere ever should. I knew enough to realize that this one, though only about the same size as I and thus relatively small as bombs go, was as nasty as they come, a fire bomb—I believe it contained phosphorus, that war's equivalent of napalm.

"Papa! Papa! Papa! Papa!" Shouting his name

23

had been the only act of which I was capable. It never occurred to me that he might be killed along with me if the bomb went off, or that he might not be able to do anything. A big, strapping man, he'd been kicked in the stomach by a mule fifteen years earlier, as a result of which he'd spent two years in the hospital, then lived the rest of his life with only a bare minimum of vital organs. When the draft had begun to take healthy men his age for the war, he said quite enthusiastically that the mule was the best friend he'd ever had. Even that "best friend" wouldn't have been able to budge the bomb, though—it was jammed tightly into the six-foot-thick, solid stone wall. None of which deterred Papa when he shoved that bomb out of his child's bedroom and to the street two stories below, where it promptly exploded. The blast burned Mrs. Schmidt's window flower boxes and further blackened walls that had already been assaulted by similar explosions, but did little other damage.

That was neither the first nor the last time I saw my father perform acts of similar caliber. Of course, he was only doing what he had to, what any good father would have done. Wartime heroism is mundane. People simply do in order to survive. At least, that's the way he tried to teach me to think. Awestruck child that I was, I was convinced my father was *Wundermann*, my own, privately invented version of Superman. Time and maturity tempered my feelings somewhat, of course, but I was still stunned, disbelieving, when he died. I mean, how could he just die like that? In his bed, of all places, like some ordinary man? Maybe he would linger after all, in the spirit.

"Coo-coo," Arnie said into my ear, bringing me out of my thoughts and back to the business at hand. Tired of poking about on the table, he settled onto my shoulder, tucked his beak into his wing feathers, and went to sleep. I didn't blame him for being tired; he'd kept me company through the rest of my night's vigil and consented to being put back into the cage only after the sun came up.

" . . . last to laugh. Halloween is my favorite holiday, though," M.A. was saying.

"There, you heard him that time, didn't you?" I said.

"Heard who?"

"Arnie, that's who. Didn't you hear him say coocoo just now?"

"Awwww, how sweet." She sipped her coffee and looked at me over the rim of her cup, which did little to hide the obvious mirth on her face. "I'm sure he did, Maa-gret."

"M.A., why won't you believe me about Arnie? How could you not believe me? Just for that, I'm going to put you to work again."

She knew I was teasing but stood up and stubbed out her cigarette anyway. We still had a long way to go before the rental trailer was empty. and if I didn't get it back to the local dealer before noon the next day, I'd be stuck with it over the weekend.

"Back into the cage with you, Arnie" I said, opening his door and nudging him toward the top perch.

He hopped onto the stick, turned around to face me, and zipped back out of the cage before I could get the door closed. Chortling in that strange combination of bird and human sound he had developed, he flew in circles around the living room, made a pass through the kitchen, then settled onto a curtain rod. With the flair of a drum major, he strutted back and forth, throwing his head proudly into the air in time to his steps.

It was an instance when I understood perfectly why some people clip birds' wings, a measure I'd never thought necessary with Arnie. Normally, he came to me as faithfully as a dog when I called him with a few whistled notes of Beethoven's Fifth Symphony. I tried a quick da-da-da-dum now, but obstinate Arnie flew to M.A. instead of to me.

With a frightened squeal, she flung up her arms, ducked her head, and covered it with her hands, almost slapping Arnie in midair.

He swerved just in time to avoid being hit, uttered his own frightened squeak, and flew directly into the cage.

"Now, what on earth was that all about?" I couldn't help shouting at her. I'd never known anyone to react in fright to Arnie before, and he had come very close to being hurt.

"I'm sorry," she said sheepishly. "It was just an automatic reaction. I've never been around a bird that flies free in the house."

"Well, don't let it happen again," I said gruffly. "He's a lot more fragile than you, you know."

We worked at unpacking the trailer until late

26

afternoon, when we ran out of objects we could handle unassisted. Things like the refrigerator and the six-foot-long freezer chest were going to require stronger muscles than ours, and I'd hired a man to come help with the heavier chores the next morning. As I'd done every night since leaving Texas, I plugged the freezer into the nearest electrical outlet.

"Thank goodness this is the last time I'll be doing this," I commented as I did so. "It's not easy making arrangements to run an extension cord from the parking lot to a motel room. Twice I had to string it across roads because I couldn't park the trailer near the room. Really had me jumpy the way cars and trucks ran over the cord all night, and I kept worrying that someone would steal everything out of the trailer—Are you all right? What's wrong, M.A.?"

Coughing and sputtering, she wiped her eyes and mouth with a napkin. "It's nothing, Maa-gret, really. I just choked on my coffee. It never dawned on me that you'd traveled all that way with food in the freezer."

"Why not? It wouldn't have made sense to let it take up that much room in the trailer otherwise. When I couldn't sell the freezer before leaving, I decided to use it for an investment. There's six hundred pounds of good Texas meat in it, all packed in dry ice. It was so hot the first couple of days on the road, though, that I turned the freezer on every night as a precaution. The beef is from the King Ranch, really superior quality."

"Maa-gret! It'll take you years to eat it all!"

"It's not just for me. I *love* to cook, you know, and this will be the first time in ages that I'll have a family around to make it worth doing again."

"A family?"

"My brother and his wife and kids. I'll have big Sunday dinners, the way my mother used to do. We'll be a real family again."

Knock. Knock. *Knock. Knock.*

"Sounds like someone's come for dinner already, Maa-gret."

I opened the front door and looked into the bright eyes of a chipmunk. Sitting on top of the mailbox, he paused but a moment to acknowledge my presence, then calmly resumed munching the acorn clutched between his upper paws. 'Hello," I said. "Are you selling encyclopedias or vacuum cleaners?" He twitched his nose, stared at me, then dropped the acorn, ran down the side of the house, and scampered away. "Just a friendly neighbor," I said as I closed the door, "but I really don't think he's the one who knocked."

Thud! Thud! *Thud! Thud!*

M.A. snapped to alert erectness on the chair. "It's coming from the bedroom!" she whispered loudly.

"Maaaaoooooooowwww." *Ka-thunk. Ka-thunk! Ka-thunk!!* "Maaow!"

"It's coming from the basement stairs." I laughed. "I closed the cats down there so they'd be out of the way while we worked." I opened the hall-way door and three miffed felines paraded through it, ignoring me as though I didn't exist. "Come get din-din," I said, trying to make peace. Sniffing at the jumble that had accumulated in the house during their banishment, they were interested in neither peace nor dinner. "Suit yourselves." I shrugged.

"He talks! He really does talk!" M.A.'s face was red with excitement, her brown eyes sparkling with amusement as she leaned over the birdcage. Arnie was in the middle of his favorite monologue. "He's a little bitty baby boy. Yes he is. Kiiiissss Arnie. He's a love. C'mere, gimme a kiss. Arnie's a sweetheart. He's a sweetie. Yes he is."

"He'll keep that up for a while now that he's started," I said smugly. "You might as well sit back and be comfortable while you listen. You know, I honestly love being able to say this—see, I told you so. He does talk!"

"I can hardly wait to tell Mother! She said you would never lie to me" She laughed. "And he's so clear! I mean, I've heard parakeets before and couldn't make out a word they were saying. Awww, Arnie, you are a love."

We had a glass of wine and talked over old times while waiting for clam chowder and stuffed quahogs to heat on the makeshift grill I'd rigged over smoldering logs in the fireplace. I wouldn't be able to get propane for the stove until the following week, just as I wouldn't have hot water until I'd fixed a ruptured radiator pipe, but this was roughing it in luxury. At least I had running water now, even if it was cold, and a load of firewood was being delivered the next morning. Once I put my things away I'd be set for the winter, for a nice, long visit with my past while I considered my future.

"You know, Maa-gret," M.A. said as she was leaving that evening, "it's strange how warm this house is after all these years. I mean, houses usually get cold and forlorn when they're vacant, but your house . . . well, it feels like someone has been living in it all along."

"She's right," I commented later as Arnie and I stared out the kitchen window. Lunar light filtered through thinning leaves; a tiny breeze ruffled them with the tenderness of a mother stroking a sleeping child's hair. It was the kind of dry, snapping cold night that makes the moon look about the size of a dime in the sky. Without a doubt, frost would glisten on the pumpkins in the morning. "Just between the two of us, Arnie, I think the house is warm because it was always so full of love, and somehow those feelings lingered, waiting for me to come back. Well, here I am." I sighed. "Here *I* am."

Arnie reached up with one foot and scratched the top of his head. "What are you doing?" he said. "I love you. Sing me a song. Sing it!" Then he began to whistle "Mary Had a Little Lamb."

"Sorry." I laughed. "But it is just you and me and the cats, kid."

Something moved out in the yard, so far off to one side that I almost missed seeing it at all. At first there was just a white blur that shimmered in the moonlight, appearing to float several inches above the ground. As I strained my eyes, trying to make it out, it began to move slowly toward me. Patiently, I waited for it to get closer so I could get a really good look. Whatever it was, it was certainly in no hurry. Inch by inch it bobbed along, stopping every few seconds, then resuming that tortuously slow progress in my direction. Abruptly, it turned and began moving toward a nearby clump of bushes.

I'd had enough of mysteries in the bedroom the night before; darned if I was going to lie awake tonight trying to puzzle out this one, too. Quickly, I turned on the porch light.

Blinded by the sudden glare, a pair of beady eyes squinted at me past a diamond-shaped white patch on the forehead. The little, pointy face that peered backward over a fuzzy shoulder held a clearly exasperated expression. A white tail marked with just a touch of black stood straight as a flagpole behind its arched, solid white back. As I watched, it danced a little jig.

"Edelweiss!" I shouted. "Arnie, it's Edelweiss. He's an old friend of the family."

And indeed he was. I had no idea how long skunks live, so maybe this one was a descendant of the original Edelweiss, but it seemed he had inhabited this neighborhood since we'd first arrived to make our home in it. I'd seen other skunks with their normal black and white markings come and go, but there had always been one around with the most distinct appearance. Three times larger than most of his kind, he was impressive enough to send all other skunks scurrying for cover when he waddled onto the scene. His stripe was so wide and unbroken, the strips of black along the sides of his belly so insignificant, that I'd thought him an albino until he allowed me to get close enough for a really good look. My father had called him Edelweiss after the velvety white alpine flower his coat brought to mind.

He seemed to stare directly at me, and I thought of opening the door, of speaking a few words of greeting to him. But Arnie was on my shoulder, and I didn't want to take a chance he might catch a draft. "Hi, Edelweiss. It's good to see you," I mouthed through the glass pane of the door instead. He lowered his tail, gave me one last look, and ambled off toward the clump of bushes, stopping every few feet to sniff at the ground.

"Looks like we'll have plenty of company outdoors, Arnie," I said. "This yard was always a naturalist's paradise. I'd almost forgotten how much I enjoyed that. C'mon. It's time for us to go to bed now."

I put him into his cage and pulled the cover around it, then lowered myself to the mattress that still occupied the floor in front of the fireplace. "Night-night. You go to sleep," he said as I crawled beneath the warm electric blanket.

"You go to sleep yourself, silly," I retorted. "I'm a grown person, and I intend to watch some television before I count sheep." Five minutes later I was sound asleep.

Five hours after that I was rudely awakened, once again, by the sound of Arnie fluttering. Mitzi crouched beside the fireplace and stared down the hallway, her ears pricked alertly, her whiskers pointing stiffly forward. Sammie stood in the hall, looking from me to the bedroom door and back again. One little clump of hair on her back stood straight up, and she appeared indecisive about whether to charge or retreat. Arnie bounced from side to side and front to back in his cage, trrrppping with great agitation. A floorboard squeaked in the bedroom.

"Not again," I grumbled, trying to get to my feet. They were immobilized as effectively as though tied to the bed by the prone form of Bundy, who was still snoring, his sleep not disturbed in the least by the goings-on. Annoyed, I pulled one of my legs from beneath him and used my foot to shove him onto the floor. He stared in surprise as I massaged my feet to get the circulation going again. "A burglar could walk off with everything in the house before I could even get out of bed," I grumbled.

A series of little thumps sounded from behind the closed bedroom door. Mitzi ran toward it, stopped short, then craned her neck to smell at the crack at the bottom of the door. Emboldened by Mitzi's initiative, Sammie trotted the few steps necessary to join her. I tagged along.

"All right, tonight we're going to get down to the bottom of this mystery." I said and flung the door open, instantly hitting the light switch.

The bedcovers were in disarray, and the lampshade tilted to one side. I had straightened both of them that morning. I had also turned the radio so I could hear it better as I worked; it was back in its original position now. I looked into the closet and beneath the bed, but there was no one in the room.

"All right, Papa, it's time for the game to end. You're scaring Arnie and the cats." I laughed nervously. "I know I'm being silly," I said to Mitzi and Sammie. "There's a perfectly logical explanation to all this. It's really a puzzle, though."

I took one last look around the room and turned to leave. Then something caught my eye, sending a chill up my spine. A bright red object lay on the floor to one side of the closet. I bent over and gingerly picked it up. It was a slipper—a man's red plaid slipper. Papa's slipper.

3 "And so, Dieter, it seems I've come home to live in a haunted house," I said.

My brother nodded, cleared his throat twice, was silent for a while, then said, "Well, the more the merrier, I guess."

He stared at me through glasses that framed his version of our father's eyes, and cleared his throat again. His lips, so like our mother's, twitched at the corners, slowly curved into a smile, then parted as he began to laugh.

"Dieter! I'm serious . . . I think."

"You've come home with a wild bird that talks . . . to a house that's haunted by our father . . . and you tell me you're serious. Don't you think I know you? Of course you're serious." He slouched down in the chair across the room from me and grinned. "Did I tell you how I won the million-dollar lottery last week? And that I've been elected president of the United States?"

I glared at him for a moment, then laughed, too. "Okay, so I'm just nervous about being back. Arnie does talk, though. You'll see."

Suddenly Dieter stood up, looking pointedly at his watch as he did so. "Well, I haven't been home yet, and it's late. I just wanted to say hello and show you where that broken radiator pipe is so you can get it fixed."

On his way to the door, he stopped in front of Arnie's cage and looked him over thoroughly. "Hi, bird," he said and whistled a tune. Arnie yanked his beak out of his wing feathers and stretched so mightily toward the sound that he appeared in imminent danger of falling off his perch. As always, my brother whistled in notes as clear and sweet as those of a nightingale.

"You should come around and give Arnie singing lessons," I said. "The big problem with his whistled songs now is that he imitates me so perfectly."

"Can I help it if I inherited all the talent in the family, while you were cursed with the peculiarities? It looks as though you haven't changed, either; still dragging home every stray animal you can find. I always meant to ask Mother if you were born in a zoo."

"Be nice! I was never that bad. Was I?"

"Weellll . . . how many other girls did we know

who brought home salamanders and tortoises and goats and—"

"Okay, okay, you've made your point. Stop now or I won't invite you over when I make roast beef and breadballs . . . Mama's way."

"That's a nasty threat, Gretel, a very nasty threat. You know—"

"Night-night. You go to sleep," Arnie said. "Night-night. You go to sleep. Night-night. Night-night. Night-night! You go to sleep. You go to sleep!"

"I think that's a hint," I said. I tried to control the smug grin that grew wider on my face as Dieter's eyebrows climbed higher on his forehead; of course, I didn't try very hard to control that grin—he had it coming.

"Wait . . . un-til . . . I . . . tell . . . Mar-tha," he said. "She loves birds, you know; feeds them all winter. Say some more, bird. Is that all he knows?"

Arnie had pulled his head into his shoulders and closed his eyes again. I was certain he wouldn't talk any more that night. "You bring Martha and the kids over for dinner when I'm settled, and you'll find out how much he says."

"That's a deal! Roast beef and breadballs, did you say? Make it soon, Gretel."

My heart was full as I watched him walk to the car. Gretel, he'd called me and, with two simple syllables, revitalized the closeness we'd shared in youth but let slip away in adulthood; no one had called me Gretel in years. I doubted if I'd ever be able to verbalize it, and I was certain my brother would be disconcerted if I did, but fear that I might never see him again was part of the reason I'd come back. I thought he was too young for the serious heart attack that had felled him last year, but if it hadn't been for bypass surgery, I wouldn't have a brother now, either. His close call had jarred me to remembrance of how dissociated I'd felt in the years when my family was a vast ocean and another culture away.

When our parents had decided to join me in the United States, Dieter would have done well to stay in Germany, where he'd already carved a niche for himself as one of the architects engaged in rebuilding the rubble pile that was postwar Munich. He came anyway. Without a grumble, he worked at menial jobs until he found employment as a draftsman, whereupon he designed countless buildings for which others were credited. It was many years before he was able to struggle his way back to accreditation as an architect in America. Now he owned his own firm and was so much in demand that he kept longer hours than a doctor. The steady determination and industry that characterized the pursuit of his goals endeared him to me almost as much as his gentle nature, quiet humor, and the fact that he'd never tattled on my many childhood mischiefs.

Cooking his favorite meal now would be a pleasure, but I couldn't handle a family gathering until I'd finished putting the house in order. That meant, among other minor details, finding places for the two beds, the extra refrigerator, and that monster of a freezer, all of which currently stood in a line along one side of the living room. As I reassembled Arnie's permanent home, a telephone-booth-sized aviary, I looked around with great dismay at the worn old furniture and drapes, the thread-bare rug, the ten-year-old paint on the walls, and I ticked off the list of necessary repairs I'd discovered with only a cursory survey of the house. "What am I doing here?" I groaned.

"Sell the house and come to Florida so you can be near us, Mumma," my daughter had urged when I'd announced I was thinking of moving back here. "There's nothing for you there anymore."

Maybe she was right, but I had to be sure before I burned the bridge behind me. This was my house, the one I'd planned, had built and worked to pay for myself after it became obvious that I could no longer live with my husband. He'd remained for a while in the big house that had been our home, then rented it to my parents and moved to the city. My life was full as I finished raising our daughter, but the inevitable day arrived when she was grown and gone. Feeling suddenly adrift, I left town in search of a cure for empty-nest syndrome. That's when my husband sold the big old family home, and I invited my parents to live in this one.

When I returned, they offered to move, but I didn't want to disrupt them again. To give us all breathing space, I built my own small apartment in the basement and settled in to live there with Mitzi and Bimpy, my half-moon conure. Though Bimpy was strictly a one-person parrot, Mitzi took immediately to my parents, who were so fond of her they actually fought over who had custody of her during certain hours of the day. She settled the dispute by being my mother's lap cat for the afternoon soap opera marathons, my father's playmate in the evening, and my frequent visitor.

I suppose I had a glorified image of myself as the dutiful daughter taking care of her elderly parents in their dotage, while they saw themselves as the loving parents once again caring for the little girl they had reared. Alas, love often creates more conflict than does hatred. We were too many parents in a home without children. The years we shared this house were warmly close ones—often fun, usually happy, yet always trying! One day I decided we all needed a break from one another, so I packed up Bimpy, reluctantly relinquished custody of Mitzi, and drove down to visit my daughter. When I pulled into Hanna's driveway several days later, she greeted me with tears and the news that my father had died the night before, less than an hour after I had last spoken to him on the telephone—and admitted to him that I planned to stay in Florida.

Together, Hanna and I flew home, where I took one look at my mother in her despair, at my father in his casket, and went into hysterics. Kindly but firmly, my daughter had put me on the first plane back to Florida. "Mumma, I understand, but Grandma is coping with all she can handle right now," she'd said. And I, rather than cope, gathered my grief into a little ball, stuffed it into a deep subconscious well, and moved restlessly from one state to another. I was in crisis, but refused to admit it. I became Margarete, the middle-aged runaway. Before my mother died, she had visited me in one place and another, and we'd finally become friends rather than merely mother and daughter. But I'd never returned home again—until now. Tired of running at last, I needed to belong somewhere.

"Let it be here," was my last wistful thought as I fell asleep on the mattress in the middle of the living room floor the third night.

For a change, my sleep was uninterrupted. Refreshed, I awoke early next morning and walked from room to room, making decisions. "Dismantle the beds," I told the hired man when he arrived. "Clear out the kitchen and bathroom cabinets. Roll up the rugs. The Salvation Army collection box will overflow this week." *I'll replace their belongings with mine*, I was thinking; *throw out the past and think only of the future.*

I went to the carpet store, selected new floor coverings, and took them home in the Blazer. Then I turned my attention to the ruptured radiator pipe. "No sense calling a plumber when I can do it myself," I decided. Digging out the blowtorch that had long been part of my homeowner's basic self-defense kit, I prepared to take care of the minor repair job. As usual, I had plenty of supervision to make certain I did everything right: Arnie perched on my shoulder and Vagabond sat at my knee; both watched my every move so intently it seemed they were trying to learn how to do the task themselves. "Pay close attention boys," I said. "You're going to

41

see an expert at work."

I reached for the pliers and began to wrench the aluminum heating fins from around the ruptured section of pipe. By the time I was ready to cut the pipe, the fins had formed a nice pile of bright, clinky objects that Arnie investigated with his beak, lifting each to look beneath it, picking it up to bang around on the floor, then throwing it to one side or another. As he pitched each piece, Vagabond batted it with his paws and pounced after it as though it were a mouse prancing across the floor.

I hummed as I screwed the pipe cutter to a snug fit. It would take no more than fifteen minutes to cut out the ruptured section and add a new piece between two fittings. "Nothing to it at all," I bragged to the animals. "I'll have hot, running water and baseboard heat for us by tonight."

My cockiness lasted about thirty seconds. The pipe was fitted so close to the wall that I couldn't swing the tool full circle to make a severing cut.

With a sigh, I sat back and stared at the problem. Bundy and Arnie ambled over, but their interest didn't last. Friend feline left my side to curl up next to his mother for a nap, while buddy bird hopped into the toolbox and began rummaging around in search of a toy. "A lot of help you two are," I said. "Bet you'd be more interested in what I'm doing if you'd had to take a cold shower, as I did last night."

I leaned forward and tugged experimentally at the pipe, then maneuvered the cutter through a couple of three-quarter turns; no, there was no way to make it go all the way around for a complete cut.

If only I could think of a way to get through that little tiny bit more of copper at the back . . . hmmmm.

Clink. Clink. Clink, clink. Clink, clink, clink, clink, clink.

"Arnie, what are you doing?" I said. He looked up at me, his expression innocent behind the piece of flat metal he clutched in his beak, then turned his attention back to the reggae rhythm he was tapping on the copper pipe. "What is that thing you have, Arnie? Let me see it."

When I reached for his drumstick, though, he ran away from me, trotting across the carpet with the gait of a jogger on stilts. "Arnold! I don't have time to play games now. That looks like something you could hurt yourself on; give it here!" I lunged toward him, and the game of chase was on. "No fair!" I protested when he flew to the top of the curtains, clutching his prize as tightly as though it were his greatest treasure and I an armed bandit. He chortled with glee when I climbed onto the couch and found I still could not reach him, then trrrppped with annoyance when I whipped the curtain back and forth, trying to dislodge him. "Oh, Arnie, please don't do this to me," I said. " I don't have time to waste on games. Please, Arnie." When I stepped down from the couch, he flew to the top of my head and dropped the object. I snatched it and saw that it was a broken piece of hacksaw blade. Arnie ran down my arm, trying to retrieve it, but he wasn't quick enough. I tossed it into the trash can.

"You're as troublesome as a baby that's just learning to walk, Arnie," I scolded. "I have to keep an eye on you constantly to make certain you don't get into mischief that's dangerous."

"He's a little bitty baby boy, yes he is," Arnie said to my wristwatch. "He's a kiss. He's a love. Kiss Arnie." He gave the crystal a couple of pecks, then started to whistle "Michael, Row the Boat Ashore."

"Hacksaw blade! Of course!!" I whirled around, retraced the steps I'd just taken, and bent to dig through the trash can. An entire hacksaw would never fit into those close quarters, but the broken piece of blade did. Using two pairs of pliers to hold it by either end, I whizzed through the rest of the pipe. A minute or two later, the replacement pieces had been fluxed and fitted. I locked Arnie into his aviary, lit the blowtorch, and soldered everything together.

I'd just leaned back to admire my handiwork when there was a knock at the front door. I opened it to greet the man I'd asked to check out the furnace and get it going. While he went about his job, I went outside and replaced the broken windowpanes in the two bedrooms.

It was a brisk autumn day, the chill wind forewarning that it would again be a cold night. This night, though, I would finally be all set in the house. The heat would be turned on, and I could take a long, hot shower before retiring. With the broken windows repaired and my king-sized bed assembled in the room that had originally been mine, I could sleep like a civilized person. That should do wonders for my nerves—calm them enough so I wouldn't be imagining noises in the night and having wild fantasies about their probable causes.

I carried the tools and ladder down to the basement and put them into the storage room, then checked up on progress with the furnace.

"Almost finished," the man said. "I'll just do a good cleaning and get a new oil filter into 'er, and she'll be good as new. Have 'er cranked up for you in less than a half hour."

I brought him a cup of coffee to sip as he worked, then looked around in the basement. It was a mess. Mama had told me about the furnace malfunction that caused the two-foot-deep flood down here, but I hadn't even begun to imagine the consequences. If my brother hadn't discovered it when he came over for lunch one day, my mother probably wouldn't have known about the water rising from below until she floated out of her bed and through the window one night. Dieter had pumped out as much as possible and drilled holes in the concrete floor to drain the rest of it, but by then everything was saturated.

In time, mold and mildew had taken over; furniture, books, curtains, walls, floors, even the ceiling were covered with green and gray fuzz. The entire basement looked like the setting for a horror movie—something called *Swamp Monster*, perhaps. It also smelled as though the monster had crawled into a corner and died in it some time ago.

"She's ready to go, lady," the furnace man said. "Looks like the old gal is in pretty good shape. I'll fill 'er now, and we'll know for sure how she's held out." He reached up and twisted the shut-off valve that would divert part of the house's cold water supply to the furnace, went upstairs to turn up the thermostat, and stood back to wait for the water to heat up and start circulating through the baseboard pipes.

The needles on the temperature and pressure gauges of the old furnace climbed steadily to positions indicating operational readiness. The roar of the flame inside its belly was as smooth as a cat's purr.

"Sounding good," the furnace man said.

With delicious anticipation, I thought of hot water droplets pelting the top of my head, my neck, my shoulders. How good it was going to feel! I could hardly wait.

"There she rips!" the furnace man said.

Gurgle, gurgle, burp, bup, bup, bup, gurgle. The water signaled its progress as it began to run into the pipes serving the heating system. *Snap, tick, tick, tick, pop, crack, crack.* The cold copper protested as it expanded with the heat for which it was the conduit. *Drip, drip, drip, trickle, trickle, splash, splosh, crash, ka-shoooossh.* The sounds of the water changed from joyful to disastrous. *Ooowwwlllll-ooorrwwwlllll.* Sammie and Bundy screamed in unison as they ran past me and pelted up the stairs. "Oh, oh," the furnace man said. Speechless, I put my hand across my forehead, using it to channel the flow of water from the top of my head away from my eyes. All around, water cascaded in great, gushing torrents from the ceiling.

"Er, I guess there was more than one ruptured pipe that needed fixing," I said.

"Yup. Looks like it," the furnace man replied as he turned off the water. He picked up his vacuum cleaner and I walked with him up the stairs and to the door. "Bye-bye. See you later," Arnie said as we walked by his cage. The man paused, looked hard at the floor, shook his head, and stepped through the door. "Give me a call again when you think you have it all set to go, lady. Sorry about flooding the basement. Not my fault, you know."

"I know," I said as he wrung out his hat. "I'm sorry about your wet clothes."

He shrugged, then smiled. "Hazards of the job. Don't worry about it. See you soon, I hope."

"How about tomorrow morning. Can you come back first thing tomorrow morning? Please!"

"Yup, I can come back then. Won't do any good, though. No way you can have it fixed that soon."

"Yes, I can. I know I can." And I hoped I could. A quick walk around the house confirmed my fear that there were ruptured pipes in every room. Water was everywhere, though rapidly disappearing as it drained through the floor to the basement below. I couldn't understand it. A plumber had been paid to drain the entire system after my mother's death; apparently he'd botched the job. Well, this time I'd do the plumbing myself and make certain it was done correctly—and quickly. I wanted that hot shower badly.

I had cut and fitted and fluxed and soldered my

way through the bathroom and both bedrooms when the commotion at the front door began. Bells and whistles and children's giggles were followed by a rap-rap-rapping of the brass knocker. Bundy and Sammie looked like one long black streak as they raced through the living room, skidded down the hallway, and dove beneath a bed. Mitzi's ears swiveled, her eyes grew large, and her whiskers pointed forward, but she stood her ground beside Arnie's cage. "Peek-a-boo. Bradddtttt, braddddtttt," he said, and crouched as low as he could get on his perch. "Trick or treat, trick or treat, trick or treat," young voices sang out from the other side of the door.

"Oh, no." How could I have forgotten? There was nothing remotely resembling a Halloween treat in the house. I dug frantically into the bottom of my purse, scrabbling for the loose change that inevitably wound up there. Witches and goblins and ghouls, cowboys and Indians and space invaders were all held at bay by nickels and dimes and quarters that night as I raced between ticks of the clock and raps on the door to repair the devastated household plumbing.

And devastated it was! My "simple" repair job turned out to be a grand total of eighteen ruptures. It was hours later before I shut off the blowtorch for the last time, satisfied that I had ferreted out and repaired all the damage.

"Well, that's that," I said. "Tomorrow I get the hot shower for certain."

I was talking to myself, though. Arnie had retired

long ago; his cage was covered for the night. And there wasn't a cat in sight, though I could hear Vagabond snoring in another part of the house. No wonder; it was late. The hands of the clock were almost aligned and pointing straight up; in another couple of minutes, it would be midnight. Come to think of it, the trick-or-treaters had quit coming to the door some time ago.

"Yes, almost midnight, on Halloween—the witching hour," I smiled to myself, remembering M.A.'s theory that my father's ghost was roaming about because I had arrived back home so near this ancient feast day for spirits. "Barbaric, heathen nonsense." I chuckled from the heights of my urbane, intellectual attitude.

I lit a cigarette and looked through the window as Edelweiss waddled across the lawn. He paused several times, sniffed at the ground, then waddled on, his head down as though in disappointment that he was finding no tasty morsels worth digging up.

Over in one corner of my kitchen, however, was an entire night's worth of tasty morsels for him. I scraped leftover cat food into an old margarine tub, turned on the outside lights, and slipped out the kitchen door. "Edelweiss, come. Come, Edelweiss," I called softly from the patio. He stopped and looked at me. I held out the dish to him, called, "Come, Edelweiss. Din-din," and set the cat food on the grass at the edge of the light's reach. He stood as still as a statue, watching me, until I went back inside the house, when he ambled over and began to eat from the dish.

Suddenly, his head jerked up. He stared toward the corner of the house, seeming to see something I could not. Then he turned, took two steps forward, and broke into a funny, rolling run that ate up surprisingly little ground for the amount of effort that seemed to be involved; a marathon runner this skunk would never be.

I laughed aloud with pleasure at the sight, remembering the game he and my father had played so often at one time: Edelweiss used to stand near the nozzle of the garden hose until Papa would go to the faucet and turn the water on; the skunk would break into that rolling run while Papa picked up the nozzle, held it high, and treated him to a shower. Goodness knows how the game started, but it was a ritual between them by the time I became privy to it, and there was no doubt in my mind that Edelweiss enjoyed it at least as much as Papa did. Seeing Edelweiss as he ran now, I could easily imagine my father out there in the yard, too, holding the hose high and laughing with glee.

Yooowwwwlllloooowwwlllllll!! Aaaarrrgghhhllll! Hiissssssss! Ooowwwllll! Hiiisssssssttt!!

"What on earth . . .? Vagabond, if you're picking on Mitzi again, you stop it right now, you hear. Vagabond!!! Samantha!!!"

I ran toward the chilling sounds of cat hysteria.

Craaasssshhhhh! Thud, thud, thud. Bump, bump. Ka-whoomp!

"Va-ga-bond!!!" I hurried my pace. It sounded like this was a serious fight rather than the usual hissing and yowling match. "Cats!" I grumbled to myself. "Can't imagine what use anyone has for cats."

The cats I had in mind almost bowled me off my feet as they exploded out of the bedroom and pounded past me down the hallway. Spitting, hissing, and bumping each other as they ran, all three acted as though they were being threatened with a bath. They were in an absolute panic.

Suddenly my steps faltered. The back of my neck prickled as the hair on it stood on end. My blood ran cold.

It was from my father's old bedroom that the cats, all three of them, had departed in such great haste. Yet, inside the room, I could still hear little bumps and shuffles, the sounds of someone—or some*thing*—moving around. It was just past midnight, on All Saints' Day, and something very strange was going on in the room where my father's body and spirit had parted company.

Swimming within the darkness framed by the doorway was a clearly visible presence. Two brightly glistening eyes glared out at me with baleful malevolence.

51

4 Disembodied eyes floating about within a darkened room. A living presence—perhaps a *not-living presence*— where none should be. Cats on the run, united in terror. Excerpts from *The Amityville Horror* and other choice haunted-house stories flashed through my mind. Instinct urged me to turn and run; to trust the cats' wisdom and beat a retreat right on their tails; to bolt through the door, herd them all into the car, and race back to Texas. I almost did it. Almost.

Then I thought of Arnie, helpless in that huge aviary, which wouldn't fit through the door, even if I could carry it. Elusive as he was, it would be risky to try to catch him. And I dared not turn him loose, not in the dark. If I fled, what was to become of Arnie? Would the presence within that room seek him out as a victim? Wring his scrawny little neck? Render him asunder? Pluck him like a duck and have him for dinner?

I could not run away.

My failure to do so went deeper than concern for Arnie, however. I must admit that actually, well, I'm not a very brave person. So it wasn't courage that made me stand my ground at that moment. It's just that I was . . . was . . . well . . . unable to move—because of paralysis. The kind of paralysis that comes from abject, cowering cowardice.

AlthoughactuallyI'mnotacowardeither, of course.

"I'm having a nervous breakdown," I said wistfully, staring hard into the darkness. The eyes gleamed out at me. "You are simply a product of my overactive imagination," I told them timorously. They winked. "I'll will you out of existence!" I said with growing confidence. The eyes squinted and moved toward me. "You are not real!" I declared. The eyes blinked, twice. "Go on, get out of this house," I ordered. "Now!!" The eyes disappeared. Clenching my fists, I waited. The darkness within the room remained, simply, darkness—devoid of light, uninterrupted by signs of movement, of life, of . . . a presence.

"Aaaaaaahhhhhhhh!" My pent-up breath exploded in the form of a relieved sigh. Sensation returned to my body, and I could move again. "It was i-ma-gi-na-tion, I know," I sang beneath my breath as I stepped toward the room. I felt separated from my body, as though I was watching a movie scene: the brave heroine walking into the jaws of the danger lurking in the dark. I'd always cringed at those scenes and called the heroine stupid for not staying in the light where it was safe. Everyone knew that danger could manifest itself only in the dark, that killers and monsters and ghosts are powerless in the light. So I flipped on the light switch, turned, and ran down the hallway.

"Good morning?" Arnie said from beneath his cage cover.

"Shhhh. You go back to sleep, Arnie. It's not morning yet." *Though I sure am going to be happy when it is,* I thought.

I reached for another cigarette, lit it, and stood at the end of the hallway, blowing smoke toward my father's bedroom. There were no sounds, no signs of movement from within. I could see the dresser and part of the bed; everything looked perfectly normal. By the time I finished the cigarette, I was feeling quite foolish. The cats had simply been fighting and chasing each other, and my nerves had supplied the eyes. "You're watching too many thrillers on TV," I mumbled to myself. "Turn out the light like a big girl, now."

Confidently, I strode the few steps to the bedroom, reached for the light switch while glancing briefly around—then banged my head on the door as I lunged backward in surprise.

There was a burglar in the room! He stood in the far corner, his hands raised as though ready to strike out, his legs poised to leap. His eyes glistened through peepholes in his mask; a black mask. His tail was ringed in black, too. And he stood less than two feet tall. My dangerous burglar, my fearsome ghost, the cause of all my late-night disturbances was packaged in the not particularly imposing body of a raccoon! I'd never been so near to one before. He looked friendly enough, but I knew he would be as skittish and ready to defend himself as any wild creature.

"Well, hello there," I said softly. Very slowly, keeping my eyes on the raccoon every second, I reached behind me and closed the door. The last thing I wanted was for him to get out of the room and force me to chase him through the house. The cats would undoubtedly get into the act then. And I had a pretty good notion how much damage that little masked rascal could do when frightened.

"So . . . how long have you been living here?" I said. My tone was conversational as I crept toward the window farthest from the corner in which he stood. "I guess you've come to think of this room as your home, haven't you?" I unlocked the window and began to inch it open. The raccoon's eyes never left mine. "And I'll bet you were pretty upset to find out you'd been locked inside when I replaced the broken window glass today, weren't you?" I reached for the spring latches on the storm window and began to ease it upward. The intruder sniffed at the crisp outdoor air that blew in. "Sorry to say so, but you're going to have to find another home after tonight. I'm certain you're too set in your ways to fit into my family, you see. Much as I sympathize with your plight, I have to look out for me and mine first. I'm sure you understand." He was beginning to look nervous as his eyes darted from me to the wide-open window.

I stepped backward as cautiously as I'd advanced across the room. When the doorknob nudged my hip, I reached for it, turned ever so slowly, and squeezed out of the room. Closing the door, I put my ear to it. Within seconds, a series of thumps marked his progress across the room; he'd taken the graceful exit offered.

I went into the bedroom and closed the window. Silhouetted in the moonlight, the raccoon sat on top of the fence and looked at me. His eyes sparked, his tail swished, and, suddenly, he was gone.

"*Auf Wiedersehen,* ghost of Papa," I said, experiencing a pang of regret.

The feeling surprised me, but it explained why I had, for a time, almost . . . well . . . believed a ghost was haunting the house. I would have liked seeing Papa—and Mama, too, for that matter—one more time, in whatever form. Just to say all the things I'd never said while they were alive, and maybe to take back some of the things I had said. To brag a little about my accomplishments since they'd gone, and to say how disappointed I was that neither had stayed around to witness everything I'd done and would be doing with the rest of my life.

"On the other hand," I murmured, "if they were around, Mama would supervise every time I used the kitchen, and Papa might not understand that his bedroom was the only place I could think of to put the freezer."

I yawned, stretched, grabbed my back with an explosive grunt as a muscle spasm gripped me between the hips, twisted, and forced me to my knees. Well, I'd known to expect the penalty of pain when I'd decided to undertake the plumbing job. My back hadn't had all its nuts and bolts since an operation years earlier, so I'd had to learn to live with the knowledge that there would always be a price to pay if I intended to keep active. Growing old is, to borrow one of my grandson's expressions, "the pits."

"If life made any sense at all," I grumbled, "the aging process would happen in reverse."

Though the backache was a constant companion in the weeks that followed, my disposition improved with each passing day. Perhaps that was partly because I was getting my full quota of sleep each night, without interruption. Life was much easier with neither ghosts nor raccoons inhabiting the quarters I refurnished and dubbed the guest room—at least, that's what it would be if I ever had a guest who was willing to sleep with a six-foot-long freezer humming motorized lullabies next to the bed throughout the night. I unpacked some of my things but relegated to the basement what I didn't need immediately. The remainder of my parents' belongings went down there, too—out of sight, safely out of mind; maybe I could sort through them later, but not now. All I wanted was to settle in enough so that I could relax and see some old friends, perhaps do a bit of baking for the holidays,

pace my days to a normal routine.

So I could ascertain whether I was here to visit or to remain.

When the first snow began to fall, I declared my chores finished for the year. With Arnie on my shoulder, I stirred steaming cider with a cinnamon stick and stared out the picture window at the lightest, most enormous flakes I'd ever seen. Large as leaves, they floated on the air, biding time patiently until the slightest breeze invited them to dance; then, with the spirit of a fandango and the grace of a waltz, they whirled and twirled, cavorting up and down, round and round, before curtsying gently to the ground. Mesmerized by their beauty, I knew that snow was another reason I'd come back. Palm trees and magnolia blossoms had courted me in my wanderings, enticing me with romantic appeal, but they'd never captured my heart as completely as landscapes cloaked in white.

"Isn't it beautiful, Arnie!" I said. "Doesn't the

very sight of snow make you want to run outside and play?"

He fluttered from my shoulder to the window sill, turned his head to the side, and peered out with one eye. Then he pecked at the glass, opening and closing his mandibles as though trying to reach out and catch a flake on his tongue. A lone ray of sunshine lanced through the leaden skies, penetrated the window, and struck Arnie full blast. Brightly illuminated. his black plumage took on the iridescent blue, purple, green sheen of an oil slick at sea. He blinked languidly, shook himself several times, squatted, tilted his head up, and slowly unfurled his wings. His beak gaped wide. Every feather on his body bristled, vibrating with the fine rapidity of a hummingbird's wings. My thoughts might be fixed on snow, but Arnie's attention had been diverted to his greatest delight—basking in the sun.

Leaving him to his pleasure, I went to the telephone and made the call I had most wanted to place since my arrival. "Hi, Dieter," I said into the receiver. "Why don't you bring the family over for dinner on Sunday. I'm finally ready for company."

I dug through my bountiful meat supply until I found the largest, most select roast. The freezer door strained at the gaskets when I shut it. That was all right; the weekly family feasts I was planning should empty the freezer quickly. On Sunday morning I whistled merrily as I seasoned the meat with a Cajun herb-and-spice blend, poured an onion-mushroom soup mix into the pan, and slid it onto the cooking rack. "Mama never did it quite like this," I confided to Arnie, "but, just between you and me, my roast and gravy are better than hers."

"Bradddttt!" he commented.

"Who asked for your opinion? Can I help it if you've sworn off meat lately? You're probably the only vegetarian starling in the world. No taste, that's what you have. Absolutely no taste!"

"Yes I do," he said. "I love you."

I stared at him, then shook my head. "Coincidence," I muttered. "The words are just sounds to him; he has no idea what they mean." Still, sometimes the things he said seemed so appropriate to the occasion that—no, no way would I let myself fall into the trap of believing the little pea-brain had enough intelligence to attach meaning to his words or mine. I might be dotty enough to talk to animals, and I sometimes responded to Arnie as though we were holding a conversation, but that was just because I'm an incurable chatterbox—none of which indicated that I was completely demented. "Sure would be fun, though," I said wistfully. "If you could converse, I mean, not if I was crazy."

He kept me company throughout my preparations, tapping around on the counter while I kneaded the breadball mixture, stealing tidbits of onion and endive as I chopped them for the potato salad, bursting into spontaneous words and whistles from time to time. The kitchen was warmed as much by my joy as by the oven's heat while I prepared that meal, and he seemed to sense it. "It'll be the best feast I've made in years," I said. "Matter of fact, it'll be the first full-fledged meal I've cooked in years. I'm so excited! I wonder if they'd come over for dinner two or three times a week. Sharing the results is what makes cooking fun."

The fun ended while I was setting the table and just as the potatoes began to boil.

A loud, sharp *Fwoop!* rattled the dishes, then a great rushing *Shhhwwwwoooooosssssssshhhhhhhhhhhh!* filled the room and did not stop.

Startled by the strange noises, Arnie leaped from the dish drainer and hurtled into the air. Flying headlong in fright, he managed to brake just short of collision with the wall behind the stove. The whooshing continued, becoming louder, more ominous by the moment. Hovering above the stove, Arnie fluttered aimlessly, his head jerking nervously in one direction, then another. The noise seemed to come from everywhere at once. Arnie could not decide which way to fly, and starlings do not hover well. Lower and lower he dangled, closer, ever closer to the boiling pot, flapping his wings with increasing agitation and decreasing lift. Horrified, I ran across the kitchen as though laboring through molasses. Arnie was well on his way to becoming starling stew by the time I reached the stove and shoved my hand beneath his falling body. Boiling bubbles flecked at my knuckles as I snatched and flung him away from the perilous pot.

He flew to the aviary and watched with passive, panting, open-beaked relief when I closed his door and locked it. "Too close, Arnie, too close," I said. "From now on, you go home before

61

the stove goes on."

I quickly followed the whooshing noise to its origin, the oven. Opening the broiler door, I peeked cautiously inside. There was no flame. Even the pilot light had gone out. Gas fumes assailed my nostrils. And the loud noise came from a fitting attached to the gas feed line. I gently closed the broiler door. Holding my breath, moving cautiously lest I do something to cause a spark, I turned the gas cock, shutting off the supply of propane to the oven. I opened windows to air out the gas, checked the clock, and groaned.

"Another hour. Just one more hour! You could have waited until the roast was done before going on the blink, you expletive-deleted oven, you!"

The potatoes boiled merrily as I gazed through the view glass of the oven door. The gravy in the bottom of the pan was dark, rich looking, and the exterior of the roast was brown. But I knew it could not be done, certainly not nearly well enough done to suit my brother's European palate. "Well, there's nothing to do but let you sit," I sighed. "Maybe the oven will retain enough heat to finish the job, and maybe Martha and the kids like their meat rare— knock on wood."

Two hours later the family of five sat at the dinner table as I pulled the roast from a barely warm oven. Despite their cheerful faces and happy chatter, from my standpoint they looked like a jury waiting to pass judgment; I'd bragged so much about this meal before the fact that I wasn't about to admit it might be less than perfect. Telling them about the oven might sound like excuse-making, I thought nervously as I began to carve. I had made more than a half dozen cuts and was beginning to breathe easier when the pink center of the flesh darkened to raw. Thinking quickly, I turned the roast around and carved from the other end until it, too, began to ooze bright red. I slipped it back into the oven, out of sight, and carried a heaped platter to the table. "See how perfect it is," I declared as I set it down with a flourish. "Well done on the out-side, medium on the inside, so everyone has a choice." I'm a great believer in the power of positive presentation.

I couldn't help noting that only well-done pieces were chosen in the first go-round of the platter.

As they ate, I chattered inanely, trying to keep their thoughts off what they were eating, hoping they weren't comparing my blunder to Mama's in-variable masterpiece—and wishing I hadn't boasted so much beforehand about my version of the meal. So intent was I on diverting their attention that I almost missed noticing the only legitimate accolade for a cook: their second helpings. "Pass the potato salad over here when you're done," fourteen-year-old David said to his mother as Martha plopped two spoonfuls onto her plate. College junior Linda and older sister Christine split another breadball and reached for the gravy boat. "Where's the beef?" Dieter asked. I gawked at the empty platter, then got up and carved from the sides of the roast.

Humming, I returned the platter to the table. Chrissie turned her head, delicately blew her nose, reached for a piece of meat, and said, "You know, Aunt Margarete, I'm surprised you haven't even mentioned your bird yet."

It was inevitable that one of them would ask, of course. Even if Dieter hadn't mentioned Arnie, that big birdcage dominating my tiny living room obviously required some explanation. Normally, I dearly loved any opportunity to spin an entertaining tale about how I came to find and raise and learn to love a common wild bird, but on this occasion I was a bit reticent. The "kids," as I still thought of my adult nieces and adolescent nephew, had grown up during a period when I'd made most of my life elsewhere; we really didn't know each other. Thoroughly steeped in the practical sensibleness of Martha's generations-old Cape Codder heritage, they might think me a bit strange.

"Dad says he can talk," David said as he rubbed his eyes.

"Dad loves to tease us," Linda explained.

"He does talk," I stated adamantly.

Bundy chose that moment to start pawing at the cellar door. The noise sounded like human knuckles rapping at the wood.

"Hear that, Linda?" Dieter said with a wink in my direction. "That's your grandfather verifying what we say. Thou shalt not doubt the word of thy father or his sister."

Bundy meowed. "It's a grandpa! It's a raccoon! It's Garfield's brother!" David said, and sneezed four times.

Realizing they'd all heard my "ghost" story, I

knew that nothing I did or said now could make me seem more odd to them. Oh, well, so what? Maybe every family should have at least one crackpot aunt. I told Arnie's tale. Carried away with enthusiasm, I walked to the aviary and opened the door. Arnie spread his wings, catapulted from his perch, and flew out. "See how friendly he is?" I said. With the pride of a doting mother, I watched him swoop through the acrobatic turns and circles he usually made around the living room. When he'd had enough exercise, he flew toward the table to check out our guests.

That's when I noticed the expressions on Martha's and Linda's faces, expressions that progressed from surprised to distressed to frightened to terrified as Arnie flew ever closer to them. My niece squealed, ducked, and looked as though she was trying to crawl under the table. Martha went white as a sheet, made a weak little cry, and threw her hands in front of her face. Realizing that he wasn't exactly being greeted with enthusiasm, Arnie slammed on his brakes in midair and dropped like a rock. He landed on top of Martha's head. She shuddered, and her hands fluttered up and down as though she couldn't decide whether to brush him off her head or keep her face protected. Arnie's eyes darted frantically as he watched her hands; his beak opened wide and remained that way; his chest heaved in and out with quick panting motions.

Moving quickly, I scooped him off her head. Sounding his starling scold, he flew to his cage and cowered for some time after I closed the door.

"I'm so sorry," Martha said. "I should have told you. Much as I love birds, it terrifies me when they fly nearby."

"Me, too," said Linda. She giggled self-consciously.

"My fault." I sighed. " I shouldn't have let him out without saying something first." I wondered at the strangeness of human nature, that any creature as large and powerful as we are could fear something as small and harmless as a bird. Then I remembered my own terror at the mere sight of a tiny spider, a phobia that even *Charlotte's Web* had done nothing to dispel. Deep in the heart of every human lurks an unreasoning fear of some innocuous creature, perhaps because we all live with subconscious dread that nature may someday lash back at us for our careless reign as the planet's dominant species.

Despite her reaction to Arnie, when we retired to the living room for coffee and conversation, Martha stood in front of the aviary, studying his every gesture, talking sweetly to him. "Generally speaking, Arnie, I dislike starlings. They're nothing but trash birds, you know, and they're always robbing my feeders. But you're kinda cute. Say something for me, hmmmm?" Exhausted by his ordeals, Arnie stared sleepy-eyed at her for a while, then tucked his beak into his wing and took a siesta. "Aw, Arnie, I meant no offense; you're no trash bird, feller." He replied with a little hiss of annoyance and snuggled his beak deeper into his feathers. "I think he's insulted," she said, turning to me.

"He seems to have disowned his family." I shrugged. "Maybe he has the same opinion of them."

She stared through the picture window, rubbed her chin, and let a slow smile brighten her face. "What a perfect setting you have for a feeding station out there. Are you going to put out bird feeders for winter?"

"I really haven't thought about it."

"Oh, you should," she said over David's and Chrissie's simultaneous sneezes. "You have no idea how much fun it is to watch the little birds in action."

As the minutes passed, my niece and nephew made more and more frequent trips to the Kleenex box. Sneezing, blowing their noses, rubbing at teary eyes, they sounded increasingly nasal when they talked.

"Catching a cold?" I finally asked.

"Allergic to the cats," David croaked.

"But I put them down cellar early this morning," I said.

Chrissie sniffed and dabbed at a reddening nose. "Doesn't matter. It's the fur; cats shed. I love cats, too, but they make me . . . *Aaahh-choo. Ah-choo. Ah-chooooo!* . . . Excuse me . . . miserable."

"I have a friend with cats," Martha said carefully. "When she knows Chrissie's coming over, she vacuums the furniture, the drapes, everything, opens her windows, and airs the house for hours before we arrive. That way, we can enjoy a nice, leisurely visit before the allergy starts to act up."

"Let's go home," Dieter said. "No reason they should be miserable."

I packed up the leftovers, keeping only the raw center of the roast, and insisted they take it all with them. "Everything was so delicious, I wouldn't dream of refusing," Martha said. "Let's meet downtown for coffee next week, okay?"

As I tucked the piece of roast back into the freezer, I surveyed its contents and sighed. " So much for the weekly family dinner. Every month or two maybe, but Dieter's right: the kids shouldn't have to suffer through a visit. And it's not in me to do spring cleaning every week. What on earth am I going to do with all this food now?"

5 "I hate December," I said, fingering my mother's wedding band. It felt strange on my hand, weighty yet worn from fifty years of contact with her flesh, but I didn't know what else to do with it. Of course, the reality that it was on my finger at all, just as our father's matching band was now on my brother's, was part of the reason I hated December. The trouble with close families is that the facts of life don't permit them to remain intact forever.

And the trouble with memories is that they can be so downright intrusive during the holiday season.

This year was particularly bad. Being back in the house we'd shared was proving far worse than I'd expected when I was down South and dreaming of a white Christmas at home. Like cobwebs, visions of Mama and Papa, of my daughter as a child, of a whole and happy family lurked in each nook and cranny of every room. Echoes of laughter—Papa's deep chuckle, Mama's coquettish-even-unto-seventy titter, Hanna's contagious giggle—were elusively just beyond the range of hearing. The imaginary scent of fruit breads baking would waft through the air at any moment if I would but allow my mind to wander at will, which I would not, for I could bear it not.

Thank goodness I had company today, and that the knock on the door had signaled one of a the few human beings to whom I would speak unabashedly when I was in this kind of mood. Responding to that knock, I'd stood there gawking at the unexpected apparition with the familiar voice that said, "I'm a bone-weary traveler seeking refuge from the storm. Is there room at your inn, madame?" Sleet whipped at the snugged-down beret and upturned coat collar of the person huddled at my door; the only visible features on the face were wind-teary eyes and the bridge of a cold-reddened nose.

"Patsy?" I said uncertainly.

"Yes, it's me, it's me! Are we going to stand here chatting or will you invite me in before I freeze to death?"

"Oh, I'm sorry!!" I stepped back, pulling at her elbow. "What a surprise! What on earth are you doing out in this weather? You're just in time to have lunch with Martha and me." *And just in time to lubricate an awkward conversation*, I thought. Like so many in-laws, Martha and I'd had our hot and cold moments over the years and were still in the process of testing the water temperature now that I was home again. So far, we'd gone through tepid and boiling, reaching for warm. This time I think we both really wanted our relationship to work, wanted to become true friends, but we were still having to work at it.

"I had an appointment in town," Patsy said as she removed her coat and hat. "Of course, I never dreamed the weather would turn so; the sun was peeping through this morning when I left home. And I didn't come for lunch, Margarete. You know me better than that."

We embraced like two old friends meeting for the first time in years—which we were. Almost thirty years old, our friendship was, dating to our daughters' grammar school days together. And, just as Hanna and Kitzi had stayed best friends over the years, so had we mothers. But Patsy had been out of town when I arrived, and we'd only made contact recently. We stood at arm's length and surveyed the damage the years had wrought. "Maybe you didn't come for lunch, but you're going to get it if I have to force-feed you," I said. "You could do with a few pounds on those bones of yours."

"All right, if you insist." She laughed. "Maybe one of your meals will help fill out these wrinkles I've acquired. You still enjoy cooking—I can tell."

"Easy guess with the pounds I've put on, huh? I go on a diet every Sunday, but then I quit smoking every Monday and that blows it all. I'm trying to persuade Martha to help me out by coming for lunch regularly, so I won't have to eat everything myself. You remember Dieter's wife, don't you?"

Humming happily, I'd prepared steak for the broiler while they renewed their acquaintanceship. The more company, the merrier, of course; maybe I could empty my freezer within the next five or six years if I had enough luncheon guests. And certainly I couldn't think of any company I'd rather have than Patsy. Dear Patsy. How close we'd always been. How many difficult times she'd seen me through. And what a lifeline she'd been to my mother after my father died. Yet, though she knew most of my intimate secrets, Patsy's private life was like a newspaper shorn down to bare-bones headlines—at least in the news section, where tragedy is always detailed. An attentive, empathic listener, she never talked about things that troubled her—except to say the few words of those bare-bones headlines.

Thus it was that I'd burbled halfway through our first telephone conversation together before she'd said, "By the way, Riki's dead. Last March. He'd finally settled down, too—gone back to school in Florida. He was on his bicycle. A car hit him." Stunned, I'd been unable to say a word. Riki was one of her two sons, the one perpetually in search of himself, of the meaning to his life. "There, now you know," she'd said. "Let's not speak of it." And though we'd conversed on the phone at least twice a day since, she'd never again so much as said his name. I had a feeling she was out in this storm today because she couldn't stand being in the house during the holiday season. But I respected her too much to violate that deep sense of privacy she had in matters emotional. Today, we'd speak of trivialities. So, in my usual tactful manner, I'd put the meal on the table, sat down, and blurted, "I hate December."

"How can you hate December?" Martha said. "Your birthday month and the Christmas holidays all rolled into one, and, so often, it's when the Jewish people celebrate Chanukah. Why, most of the world is jubilant in December! It's the most joyful month of the year."

"Holidays are why I hate it," I said. "They're so depressing."

Martha paused in midbite, staring at me over her fork. "You don't seem to have the right attitude about the holidays, Margarete. They're supposed to be happy, festive, a time for caring and sharing with those you love."

"Bah! Humbug!!"

"Why don't we go shopping together next week. That'll cheer you up."

"Let me guess," Patsy said with a twinkle. "You've heard from Hanna, right? They've changed their minds about coming home for Christmas, right?"

I sighed, "Right. Travie's father won't let him come. The court says Christmas Eve is Travie's holiday with him, and that's that. Guess I shouldn't complain. At least he wants to spend time with his son, which is more than many fathers do in these divorce cases. Still, I can't help wishing that grandparents had some rights, too; but I guess children are already torn in too many directions by these things. Now what am I going to do with the five thousand cookies and dozen fruitcakes I baked?"

"You can bring some of them to our house on Christmas night," Martha said. "And if you freeze them, you could bring some more next year; and the year after that; and every year until they're all eaten." We laughed at my foolishness and the luncheon mood lightened, at least until Martha had gone. When I decide to get gloomy, there's no stopping me for long until I've worked it out of my system, and Patsy knows me well enough to realize that usually means I need to hear myself talk it through. Verbal as I am, I often talk in circles when I'm distressed, but there are few to whom I'll say what's really on my mind. Gently, my closest friend led me back to the topic.

"You have a Christmas invitation; you won't be alone, Margarete."

"I know. Christmas night is her family's traditional get-together; her father, sisters, brothers-in-law, nieces, and nephews will be there. She said to consider myself an extension of her family. A nice gesture, but how can I feel like family with people I've only met briefly?"

"By getting to know them, of course. You've never been reluctant about mingling with new people, though, Margarete, and you've spent the holidays without Hanna before. What is it?"

"It's being in this house right now. I should have

sold it and never come back. The memories are killing me!"

"No, they're not." Patsy's mouth twitched with a sad little knowing smile. This was a widow I was talking to, a woman who sorely missed her adored husband to this day. Still, she'd carried on with the rearing and support of their children, the maintenance of the huge family home after Herman's death. Though her other son, Fritz, lived in the former "in-law quarters," Patsy had been essentially alone for years, alone with her houseful of memories. Yes, it was a knowing—and humbling—smile that preceded her softly spoken sage observation, "Memories may hurt, but they don't kill. When grief won't let you remember, that's when part of you is dying. Healing doesn't begin until the memories can flow; it's about time for you. Don't fight it, Margarete; you're starting to heal."

"Healing shouldn't hurt so much, if that's what it is," I mumbled later as I stared at the boxes of cookies and the row of foil-wrapped cakes on the breakfast bar. Near them was the Christmas goose platter Mama had given to me one wedding anniversary after deciding the marriage she'd so opposed was going to last. Her own mother had passed it on to her under similar circumstances, just as I would someday present it to Hanna. A daughter's rite-of passage symbol, that platter. Too bad it was going to remain unused this year, again.

"I'm just not going to hold Christmas!" I shouted. In a fit of pique, I snatched up Mama's tattered old holiday cookbook and tossed it into the trash.

"In fact, I'm going to cancel Christmas from now on. Scrooge had the right idea. Bah! Humbug!!"

I stomped out of the kitchen and glared through the window at the snow that was beginning to cover the ground. Looked like it was going to be a white Christmas, just as I'd wanted—for those celebrating it, anyway. In the view from my window, the world seemed limited to the first few feet of my front yard. Beyond that, I could occasionally make out the hedges as a vague blob when wind gusts wiped the thickly falling flakes to one side or another, but nothing else. I was isolated, with only my morbid thoughts for company.

"Peek-a-boo. Hi there, coo-coo," said a raspy voice near my ear.

Correction—I was isolated with only my thoughts, the cats, and, of course, Arnie for company. And he was the greatest cure for melancholy I'd run across in many a year. "Come out here and help me get rid of my December blues, Arnie," I said, opening the aviary door. "I'm feeling so sorry for myself. Do you think you could give a good, swift kick to bring me to my senses?"

"Kissy, kissy," that silly starling said. He flew from his perch and landed on my shoulder. "C'mere, you gimme a kiss."

"No, no, not a kiss, a kick, I said. Give me a kick, so I'll quit wallowing in my misery."

"You're a baboon," he scolded and took a nip at my earlobe. "What are you doing?"

"Taking a mental walk with the Ghost of Christmas Past, that's what I'm doing." I sighed again.

"You know, when I was a little girl in Munich, we always started celebrating the holidays on my birthday. My brother and I spent all of December fifth waiting for Sankt Nikolaus to show up at our door at five o'clock, and the wait was always an anxious one because of Knecht Ruprecht."

A powerful sense of déjà vu gripped me as I stood at the window. The accumulating snow, the steadily falling, fine flakes I was watching, had always been part of the Munich scenery this time of year, too. And just as Arnie clutched my shoulder now, Medie's little parakeet talons had gripped me then. I could almost hear Dieter's young voice in my ear. "My knees hurt, Gretel; how long are we going to kneel at the window?"

"Ssshhhh! I'm listening. And trying to figure out what I'm going to do. Mama says I've been a bad girl this year, that Knecht Ruprecht might stuff me into his sack and carry me away. You won't let that happen, will you, Dieter? You'll help me hide if mean old Ruprecht tries to take me, won't you?"

He put his arm around me, patted me on the back, and asked tremulously, "But won't he put me into the sack too?"

"Not if I tell him that I picked Mrs. Schmidt's flowers, and that I'm the one who makes you giggle when we're supposed to be asleep, and that it was my idea to feed Sunday's schnitzel to the dog."

"That's true, but I got punished for those things, too. Will Ruprecht believe—"

"Ssshhhh! Listen! Is that Sankt Nikolaus's bells ringing? And Ruprecht's chains clanging? They're coming! I can hear them on our block already!!"

Like children all over Germany, we listened with bated breath, aflutter with excitement, atremble with simultaneous fear, as we awaited the judgment that was part of every *Sankt Nikolaus Abend*. For good children were rewarded with sweets by the kindly bishop, while naughty ones were said to disappear into rotten Ruprecht's sack, perhaps never to return home. The jingle of merry bells was carried on the wind—as was the jangle of Ruprecht's chains dragging—and occasional flashes of red were seen as doors of first one apartment building, then another, opened and closed. Sankt Nikolaus, *Der Weihnachtsmann,* was on his way to our home, but so was his helper, Knecht Ruprecht. And my brother and I were seldom so very close as when we awaited our annual judgment day.

Mentally, we tabulated our good deeds and our bad as the first steps sounded at the bottom of the stairs. Clinging tightly to each other, with Medie hopping from my shoulder to his and back again, Dieter and I listened to heavy, thudding footsteps drawing nearer, ever nearer, until the loud *Knock! Knock! Knock!* rattled our own door. Hand in hand, we walked what seemed a thousand miles to open it.

And there they stood. The white-bearded bishop in flowing red vestments held the curved scepter of his office in one hand—and a long list in the other. At his shoulder was Ruprecht in rags, a scraggly image of dirty gray and black, the sacks of his function clutched tightly in either hand. "Margerete

Maria Katherina Theresa Sigl," Sankt Nikolaus intoned from his list. "You stole Mrs. Schmidt's flowers, didn't you?" On and on he droned, seeming to have witnessed every misdeed of which I'd been guilty throughout the year. Surely I will not escape Ruprecht's revenge this year, I worried. Nor would Dieter, it seemed, when his list was read.

"How do you know so much?" I was bold enough to challenge when the indictment was done.

"Sankt Nikolaus knows all," he said sternly. "I think you should stuff them both into the sack, Ruprecht."

"No, please don't," we cried in unison. "We'll be good as angels next year. Could you spare maybe one little *Lebkuchen* for each of us if we promise to reform?"

"Fortunately, we were very persuasive," I said to Arnie with a chuckle. "Otherwise, I wouldn't be here now, and you would've died when you fell from your nest without me around to rescue you."

"Peek-a-boo. I love you, yes I do!" he said.

"If you love me, little rascal, I must have grown up to have some redeeming qualities, huh? Maybe Sankt Nikolaus could see into the future and realized that would happen. You can imagine my surprise when I arrived in this country and discovered that it takes Sankt Nikolaus almost three weeks to travel to America and that on the way he changes both his clothes and his name. I haven't met many people who even know that Santa Claus is a bishop in disguise. I'll bet he wouldn't get away with that trick if he brought Ruprecht with him instead of the reindeer and elves he picks up along the way. Silly holiday, Christmas. I should have quit celebrating it long ago."

There was a loud crash in the kitchen. The three cats leaped from individual sleeping posts about the room and raced ahead of me to investigate the noise. A beer stein I'd given Papa one Christmas was shattered all over the breakfast bar. Ruefully, I looked at the knickknack shelf upon which it had stood; everything else there seemed to be solidly in place. It wasn't until I started picking up the pieces, however, that I noticed the greater loss: beneath the heavy base of the broken stein, the goose platter lay in two exact halves, the line dividing them looking as neatly drawn as though it had been measured and cut with a diamond. I paused over the trash can— and fished out the cookbook before dropping in the broken pieces of stein. The platter I tucked away; maybe it would still hold a goose after it was glued back together.

That night I dreamed of Sankt Nikolaus and Ruprecht standing at my door. Behind them Mama and Papa were shaking their heads sadly. "Gretel, Gretel," they said in unison, "how could you forsake the one holiday that means everything to us? Even if only in spirit, we've always been together, a family, for Christmas. We never thought you'd desert us this way." Nikolaus looked to my shoulder, then to Ruprecht's sack. " She's too big for the sack now," he said. "But she's lost her sense of wonder and deserves to be punished. If she doesn't understand what Christmas is about, how can she appreciate something as remarkable as a talking starling? Take the bird, Ruprecht; put Arnie into your sack. My elves will give him to someone who delights in the little joys that add up to happiness."

I woke up crying. "Silly, childish dream for a grown person to have," I grumbled as I swiped at the tears with a tissue. So silly, so childish, so disturbing that this grown person couldn't go back to sleep, fearful of another nightmare, undoubtedly. I wasn't feeling very secure in my adulthood at that point. So I lay there remembering Decembers of my youth.

How bright and shining Munich had been with all its merry lights. Ice statues had adorned even little neighborhood parks, and every large department store window had been alive with mechanized fairy tale figures. Living in the Schwabing section of Munich as we did, we had many Jewish friends and neighbors who added significantly to the spirit of our Christian celebration during their Chanukah; to all of my playmates, children being as simple and naturally rational as they are, December was the universally joyful month when *everyone* celebrated with light, lights, lights, lights!

Our parents saved all the year long to be certain the *Christkindel* would bring many wonderful gifts for Dieter and me on *Weihnachtsabend*. And our grandfather, who was a forest warden, always made a hundred-kilometer round trip on the train each December twenty-fourth to bring us a freshly cut blue spruce. While my brother and I sipped punch and nibbled cookies in the kitchen that evening, the tree would be decorated and presents laid out in our large dining room. When all was in readiness, my parents turned out the lights and jingled a bell. In response to the signal, we children lit candles to guide our way down the long hallway. Step by slow step, we walked hand in hand and sang *"Stille Nacht, heilige Nacht, alles schlaft, einsam wacht . . . "* on our procession to that transformed room . . . transformed because of the wondrous tree, all aglow with tiny lit candles and bright, spitting sparklers.

The lights went out in Munich just as they did in cities worldwide during the war, of course, but the blackout was never so dismally dark as it was during December. Friends and relatives alike began to be lost in ever so many ways. Certainly there couldn't be treats from Sankt Nikolaus when there were food shortages, nor wonderful gifts for children when the factories were all so busy making weapons and uniforms and other supplies for the war. Yet, behind our thick curtains, my parents still managed the moment of wonder that was our first sight of that Christmas tree—except for the year we spent Christmas Eve in the bomb shelter, that is—a false alarm that nevertheless canceled the entire event. The year after that our grandfather was no longer alive, and there was no tree. Still, even in the worst of times, my parents always found some way to celebrate what they regarded as *the* family holiday.

As I would do this year, too. How could I not after a night like that, with memories more acutely haunting than any nightmare could possibly be?

While I was under the basement stairs digging through boxes in search of tree decorations, one single item clattered to the cement floor. Hesitantly, I picked it up and tenderly stroked its wooden base, its bristly body. My father's clothes brush. How often it had been gripped by his hand, as he cared for the elegant suits crowding his closet.

In Germany there was never a day when I didn't see my father in one of those suits. An executive with a Swiss construction company, he'd always taken great pride in his appearance. Something of a dandy in his own way, I suppose he was, and so proud of my mother in the designer dresses he regarded as appropriate for her beauty and the station he'd achieved in life. Past the age of fifty when he immigrated, he never did learn to speak his new tongue very well, which made it impossible for him to be an executive of anything in this country. So after he arrived in America, he wore a suit on only two occasions—no, three: when he was sworn in as a citizen, when my brother got married, and in his coffin. For men who collect garbage, paint houses, and serve as school custodians don't wear suits from day to day. Even so, he faithfully cared for his unfashionable, dated, but still-elegant German suits, stroking each and every one, each and every week, with that clothes brush, in the privacy of his bedroom.

He complained only once: when my mother went to work as a seamstress. In her feisty way, she stilled his tongue with the short, sharp words, "It's for the Christmas money. We came here so we could be a

family together. And this family will always have a grand Christmas, Johann. Always!"

Letting the memories flow, I lugged the decorations upstairs and called Martha. "I know you've been doing things differently in recent years, but don't you think it would be nice if we go back to the old tradition of a family Christmas Eve here?"

"Thank goodness! We were beginning to worry that you weren't going to ask us, Margarete. Of course! It'll be Christmas Eve at your place—will you make your potato salad for us?—and Christmas night over here. This is going to be the best Christmas we've had in years!"

"Sure hope Patsy's right about memories being part of the process of healing grief," I said as the animals helped me decorate the tree and wrap gifts, "because I'm certainly having more than my share of them this month."

"Good!" Arnie said, diverting his attention from the bow he was trying to rip off one package. Sammie watched his efforts, occasionally nudging with her nose at the unyielding bow, which I pulled off and tossed into the middle of the floor. While Sammie and Bundy attacked it, Arnie flew to a window and whistled "Mary Had a Little Lamb." Strange— it sounded remarkably like the "Jingle Bells" playing on the radio.

When I'd finished with the packages, I went around to the neighbors' houses, wishing them happy holidays—and foisting off some of my excess baked goods. Polite people all, they accepted them as magnanimous gifts. Which gave me a conniving, sneaky idea of one way I could satisfy my cooking urges and eventually empty that freezer. Neighbors are nice people with whom to share.

The telephone rang as I walked back into the house. "Mumma," Hanna said when I picked it up, "I've been thinking . . . since we're not coming for Christmas, suppose I send Travie to you for spring vacation? By the way, I think I've decided to marry Ronnie . . . about this time next year. Then we'll all come home for a long summer vacation."

Ah, well, life does have a way of working out if we simply allow it to. Families change as people come and go within them, but without change, there would be no life.

On Christmas night at my new extended family's house, my nephew squeezed my right hand while my brother embraced me from the left. In their dining room, a group of wonderful people stood in a circle round the table, holding hands and singing "Silent night, holy night, all is calm, all is bright . . . " That is, everyone but two in the circle sang it—my brother and I belted out the words *"Stille Nacht, heilige Nacht, alles schlaft, einsam wacht . . . "* To the same tune, of course.

6 *Ooooooohhhhooooowwwwwwwllooooohhoooooooow-wwwllllllooohhhooowwll.*

I shivered, put down the paint roller I was using on the living room ceiling, and pulled my sweater closer around me. When the wind whistled down the chimney that way, the cold cut right to the marrow of my bones. This was a winter Mother Nature had fabricated to try everyone's endurance. For the first time in memory, the ocean was frozen so solid that it was possible to walk all seven miles from the Falmouth Heights beach to Martha's Vineyard, and the ferry that usually made supply runs to the island from Wood's Hole was solidly stuck in the Sound, awaiting rescue by a Coast Guard icebreaker.

Yet, in his cage, Arnie was singing so happily that I had to wonder if he thought it was spring. Considering the fact that I had dragged him north for the winter, a move so contrary to a bird's nature, I wouldn't be the least bit surprised if he did have his seasons all mixed up. On the other hand, there was a great deal about which he should be happy. After all, he wasn't outside, having to endure the effects of that winter.

Each time I watched his fellows, I felt like inviting them all in for a visit—a long visit, say, until the ground thawed. The weather was brutalizing the birds. After each new temperature plunge, there were obviously fewer of them. The survivors hopped about on one foot, keeping the other tucked tightly into wing feathers for warmth, then alternating in order to warm the exposed one. They switched so often from one foot to the other that I was certain their toes must hurt from the cold.

"I'm really glad you don't have to be out there, Arnie," I said as I looked out the window. "I wish none of the other birds had to either. If I were filthy rich, I'd turn my entire back yard into a solar-heated aviary so the birds could fly in and out to warm up during the winter months."

"Coo-coo," Arnie said.

"Now you be nice! If not for you, I wouldn't be noticing the birds as much as I do, and I wouldn't feel so bad about their situation."

"I love you," he soothed.

"Hmmph! You should have thought of that before insulting me."

"Bad boy!" he said in the exact tone I used to reprimand Bundy.

Turning back to my view of the outdoors, I shivered again. The old, familiar scenes to which I was long accustomed resembled alien landscapes carved from ice. Even the sunlight looked cold lately. It was a bright winter, not one of those dark, gloomy ones marked by too many clouded days, but something about the extreme low temperatures changed the very character of the light outside. A large but pale sun climbed the horizon each day, illuminating the earth with a strange blue light, but not warming it.

Among the needles of the spruce tree flanking the driveway, a chickadee hung upside down from the thistle stocking, his black-capped head bobbing rapidly as he pecked at the last seed in the bottom. A hole gaped a few inches above his clinging talons, evidence that the squirrels had been busy again. Most of the tiny seeds lay scattered on the ground, shiny specks glistening like black sequins on top of the frozen snow.

House sparrows nibbled at it, though in a desultory manner. Lying on their bellies in the snow, they looked as though they were eating only because the food was right under their beaks, not because they were particularly hungry. Well, who invited them to the party, anyway? I'd never intended to feed so many common birds when I put up my feeders. I was more interested in the tiny titmice and finches and nuthatches and such that were less numerous and more difficult to attract. Sparrows, indeed; they were a dime a dozen.

"Bad boy, bad, bad, bad boy," Arnie said again as a loud banging and clattering noise drew my attention suddenly to the window on the south side of the living room. On top of the television set, Bundy and Sammie stood shoulder to shoulder with whiskers twitching and tails swishing mightily from side to side as they pushed their noses against one of the glass panes. Arnie trrrrpppped in annoyance and pecked at the side of his cage. My savage starling and two attack cats always managed to put on a good show of protecting their territory—as long as they were safely indoors and the intruder was outside. I walked over and rapped on the window.

About six inches from Bundy's nose, a large ebony grackle clung with the tips of his talons to the wire rim of a feeder designed to accommodate birds one-quarter his size. He looked at me unflinchingly with tiny yellow eyes that seemed to acknowledge my rapping as a greeting rather than a signal that he was unwelcome. He blinked once, and seeming satisfied that he'd paid his respects as a good guest should, he leaned back, flapped his wings for balance, and proceeded to empty the feeder with great, gobbling mouthfuls. As he ate and flapped, the feeder swung to and fro on the wire by which it was suspended, banging heavily into the side of the house. More seeds fell to the ground than the grackle managed to get into his beak. He glanced up for a moment when I rapped on the window again, but didn't leave until he'd had his fill.

"Darn grackles," I grumbled. "They're as bad as

the sparrows and starlings about emptying my feeders! No offense to you, Arnie. It's just that they waste so much food that might otherwise keep the pretty little birds from starving to death this time of year."

As the grackle disappeared over the roof of April's house, my attention turned to the half dozen starlings sitting on the pile of brush I was using as kindling. What fat little beasties they were, thanks, no doubt, to the feed they managed to steal from the other birds; but how cold they looked! They sat on their feet instead of perching upright and had their heads drawn tightly down into their necks. The capricious, icy wind ruffled their plumped feathers first to one side of their bodies, then the other. As I watched, one of the birds suddenly lurched forward and fell to the ground, where it lay on its back—unmoving.

Without thinking to grab coat or boots, I ran outside. Every bird in the yard scattered at my approach—every bird except the fallen starling. I scooped him up and carried him into the house, thinking that warmth would soon bring him around.

Cupping him with both hands, I thought of how I would revive him, give him a nice meal, then let him go so he could rejoin his family outdoors. Poor baby was freezing cold to the touch. I blew gently into the space between my thumbs, hoping that the warmth of my breath would help thaw him quickly. Maybe I wouldn't send him back outside after all; maybe he didn't have a family to miss him; maybe

I'd adopt him until spring; maybe he and Arnie would strike up a friendship, and I'd never send him back outside. That was it. I would save his life, just as I had done with Arnie, and then I'd make him, too, a part of my little family.

"C'mon, little starling, wake up. It's nice and warm in here—feel it? Arnie, say something to him, to let him know he's among friends. Listen, little starling, I have a bright and wonderful future planned for you. You don't have to go back into that ugly weather outside, not ever again if you don't want to. Wake up now; wake up."

It wouldn't have mattered if he were a chickadee or a cardinal or a finch or a grackle at that moment. I was going to save him. Again and again I blew into my hands. Softly, I whistled between my teeth in tones to which Arnie had always responded. I earnestly begged him to wake up. I rubbed his tiny body, ever so gently, trying to restore circulation.

Shocked, I realized that this was not the fat little bird I had thought him to be. His breastbone jutted from his feathers like the ridgepole of a tent; to both sides of it, his chest was caved in so much it was difficult to imagine there was even a ribcage within his fleshless little body. On close examination, he was nothing but bones and feathers held together by the thinnest covering of skin imaginable. His eyes remained open and glazed. I was too late to save him. Worst of all, the horrible truth slowly dawned on me—he had starved to death, and that was something I could have prevented.

"Awww. See what I mean, Arnie? That's really a

cruel world out there. And here I've been begrudging the bird seed he managed to steal. Poor baby. He deserved a chance to live as much as the other birds I chose to feed."

Arnie fell silent at my words and stared through his screening at the sight of me sitting in my chair with the dead starling cradled in the palm of my hand. He cocked his head first to one side, then the other, and uttered uncharacteristic little peeping noises.

"Well, what was I to do," I said defensively. "It would take tons of bird seed to feed them all."

Arnie hopped down his ladder of perches to the bottom of the cage and began gobbling corn as though it was going to be yanked from beneath his beak at any moment. Seeming heavier by the moment, his dead wild cousin lay like a lump of guilty conscience in the palm of my hand.

The feeder banged and clattered against the side of the house. It was a grackle again, gobbling what he could before losing his precarious balance on that contraption designed strictly for small birds. I didn't try to chase him away. On the ground, mourning doves and juncos and blue jays and sparrows and the dead starling's relatives vied for every crumb they could snatch of the seeds the grackle spilled.

I wrapped the dead bird in a paper towel. It was impossible to bury him; the ground must be frozen down to at least a couple of feet beneath the surface. "I'll start throwing out bread for your relatives, little starling." I promised as I placed him, with utmost tenderness, into my garbage can. I paused for a moment and looked at him in his blue-flowered paper shroud. He lay among the empty cans and discarded paper wrappings that represented the abundant food supply of my own household. Scattered about his body were the corn kernels and cat food and table scraps that Arnie and the cats and I invariably left behind after we'd eaten our fill.

I went back to my painting and settled in to some deep thinking. I had put out the feeders strictly for my own entertainment, with little thought of altruism, hadn't I? I had determined to feed a few select kinds of birds without regard for the genuine needs of any of them, hadn't I? That was something like setting up a soup line and putting out a sign saying that only rosy-cheeked, smiling, witty children need apply, wasn't it? Did that make me a bird-lover? Or did that earn me the label of bird-bigot? The faster my thoughts ran, the faster I painted. Much as I needed to get on with the rejuvenation of the house, there was something much more pressing on my agenda at that point.

Finished early with that day's work, I put away my tools and paint as quickly as possible, went down to the basement storage room, and dug out a flower pot and a bag of potting soil. At the kitchen sink, I filled the pot half full and put the bag with the remaining soil handily on the countertop. Then I reached down into the garbage can, removed the body of the dead starling, laid it on top of the dirt in the flower pot, and finished filling it with soil from the bag.

Bundy, posted in front of his food dish, watched with the creases of a frown between his eyes.

"I'll get to you in a minute, Bundy," I said, "but I have to do this first. I know I'm being silly, but he does look exactly like Arnie. I don't think I'd be able to sleep tonight if I had to keep thinking of him being thrown away like ordinary garbage."

It was a bit unorthodox to inter a bird in a flower pot, I suppose, but it would have to do for now. I carried the pot outside and put it into the ash can. It was the perfect place to keep the bird's body in cold storage. When the ground thawed enough to be shoveled, I'd give him a proper burial. Silly or not, it would make me feel better.

Returning to the warmth of the house, I closed the kitchen door against the cold, gusty wind. Now all three cats were sitting in front of dishes that still held the substantial but dried-out remnants of that morning's feeding. "It's obscene how much food gets wasted around this house when there are starving creatures all around us," I grumbled as I picked up the bowls. I took a covered dish from the cupboard, snapped off the plastic lid with a flourish, and made a great ceremony of emptying the leftover cat food into the storage container. "There will be no more food wasted from this household, not ever again," I growled as I glared at the cats and opened a fresh can of tuna. "There are going to be some changes made around here, *start-ing to-day!* From now on, every crumb will be eaten. Every crumb!"

"Da-da-da-dum!" Arnie whistled.

I dished out the tuna. "Anyone who wants to eat better start now." I said. "And I do mean now!" Three pairs of widened feline eyes stared at me with bewilderment. "Eat!" I commanded. Three furry heads ducked, quickly. Loud smacking noises assured me that I was the boss of the household—for now.

I went to Arnie's cage, opened the door, and walked to the bookcase. Arnie fluttered after me, landed on my shoulder, then hopped to the nearest shelf, looking at each book in turn as though searching for a title to his liking.

"I know the cat food's ideal, Arnie," I said, "because M.A. has complained a number of times about the birds stealing her cats' dinner when she serves it outside. It's time for me to do some homework, though. If I expect the birds to entertain me, the least I can do is establish a proper feeding program for them."

The book I was looking for had been my favorite Christmas present this year, actually, but I'd busied myself with other things and never gotten around to using it. I was ashamed of myself for not yet having explored its pages. Well, now I intended to remedy the situation. I found the book and pulled it from the shelf.

Arnie followed me to my easy chair and paraded up and down the arm until I was settled. Then he perched on my wrist and used his beak to help me turn the pages as I began to leaf through *A Complete Guide to Bird Feeding*. "We'll know how 'complete' this is, won't we, Arnie, when we see if this John V. Dennis bothered to mention starlings when he wrote his guide."

My doubts were quickly dispelled. The book's index listed starlings specifically, with many references to them throughout its page. What's more, starlings were presented in the most balanced fashion I had yet encountered in any written reference. Just as the text advised ways to outwit starlings for those who didn't share my fondness for the controversial bird, it also gave a wonderful list of foods that are their favorites. I even learned that I could feed the several varieties of "trash" birds including the grackles and house sparrows, enough to help them through the brutal winter months without causing any hardship to the more favored little birds and that, in all probability, once the weather broke, most of the "nuisance" birds would return to their natural food sources with no urging from me.

"Do you see that long list of starling favorite foods, Arnie?" I said. "Things like rice and potatoes, cheese and bread and corn. Why, basically, it's all table scraps!"

"Braddddtttt!" Arnie said.

"No one asked you. Your canned corn and eggs are on the list, too, but basically I'd say you're just too downright particular—very unstarlinglike of you, you know. I think I'll put you on a new diet—say, dog food and sauerkraut and, let's see, how about some good, fresh suet. Sound appealing to you?"

"Kiiiisss Arnie," he said. "He's a little bitty baby boy, yes he is. I love you, yes I do."

"You think sweet talk will get you off the hook, do you? Well, I'll think about it. Maybe a day or two outside would convince you to eat whatever I serve you."

He began a quiet rendition of "Mary Had a Little Lamb." If the sweet talk wouldn't dissuade me from being so grouchy, perhaps a soothing serenade would.

Ever so cautiously, Bundy peeped around the corner, looking at me with his most appealing little-kitten expression. "Come on, Bundy," I invited, patting my lap. He jumped up, licked my hand, and stretched out with a loud purr. Sammie was right behind him, sneaking to her position alongside her son as though hoping I wouldn't notice her presence. Mitzi took the post atop the back of the chair. She didn't flinch a whisker when Arnie hopped onto her back and started parting her fur with his beak.

"I'm not mad at any of you, you know. I'm mad at myself for having been so thoughtless. Every day

I throw away food that could get a lot of wild birds over the hump in this kind of weather. The snow and ice have covered all their natural foods. We have to help them. We have to!"

Mentally, I started to tick off the little things I could have been doing all along, if I had only thought. Why, many of the birds resorted to the bird seed only out of desperation, because there simply was nothing else on which they could survive. They were freezing and starving out there while we were so snug and well fed in here.

And I knew, oh, how well I knew, what it's like to starve. How well I remembered my years as a teenager in a Europe racked by famine after the war: how I'd relished a "soup" made of rotten onions and water and Mama's love; how I'd climbed a mountain with a friend to cajole one pat of butter from a milkmaid to split between the two of us; how I'd been beaten for picking a green apple from a farmer's tree; how my father had risked his life to salvage a crate fallen off a supply truck in the belief it was food—and how disappointed we'd all been to discover it was a box of lice combs. I, too, would have fought for a handful of sunflower seeds back then.

Because starvation hurts. Not with a mere knawing in the belly, which is a symptom of simple hunger. Starvation is an acid that eats away at the bone and muscle and nerve endings and soul until the entire body is afire with pain, the mind numb to all else. Every human being on earth is only forty-five days away from that fate at any given time of the year; and that grace period applies only if the machinery of food distribution proceeds unhampered by greed, selfishness, and downright ineptness. Except for the predators, animals would not survive a fraction of that time should plant life cease to grow tomorrow; and starvation nips at their heels much closer, more constantly than at ours, giving them pain that is stoically endured but no less real than that felt by the human animal.

Maybe starvation's subconscious haunting memory/fear is the reason I have such a passionate interest in cooking, though it was not always so.

As a young child, I paid no heed to Mama's attempts to teach me the culinary arts because I had too many other ambitions—Olympic gold medalist, actress, opera star, doctor, race car driver, queen of a country that didn't need soldiers. I was going to be all that and more. Mature self-sufficiency was forced on me, as war has a way of doing to children. So when I was fortunate enough to marry a kind, older man willing to spoil me, I quickly reverted to childhood irresponsibility. Why should I learn to cook when he so obviously enjoyed doing it himself, when I could be out playing baseball until he called me to dinner? Frank had thought ours the perfect arrangement, as had I.

The U.S. Army was oblivious to our marital bliss, however; they shipped Frank off to another war, this time in Korea. And there was I, responsible for nurturing a growing little girl, yet incapable of properly toasting a slice of bread. "This is how you use a can opener." Frank hastily instructed as we packed his duffel bag. "The two of you can survive on pork and beans until I get back."

"I can live on Mounds bars and blueberry pie," said Hanna quite cheerfully.

"The shame of it," my mama wailed over the telephone. "To think I'm afflicted with a daughter who can't cook! Come home. Live with Papa and me so the baby won't starve."

And be treated like a baby again myself? Never! I thought. "I'll learn," I said.

And Hanna and I quietly began eating out. Restaurant food that had been tasty when novel, though, soon became blandly boring.

"I'd trade a whole blueberry pie for some of Daddy's spaghetti sauce," Hanna said longingly one day. Frowning over the untouched hamburger on her plate, she was creating catsup art on a napkin with one of her cold french fries.

"Then let's go home and make some," I said, standing up and taking her by the hand. "Everything's at home in the cabinet; between us, we'll figure out how to put it together right."

Just as necessity is the mother of invention, desperation is the father of inspiration. And desperate is the only way to describe a pampered palate suffering from home cooking withdrawal symptoms. The very first sauce created by my four-year-old daughter and me was so inspired that I was certain my Italian-born husband would proudly serve it to his Sicilian family. I've always thought our laughter as we worked was the secret ingredient that went into the pot that long-ago day. Or perhaps the secret ingredient was the love growing in my heart for, indeed, I found a new love while my husband was in Korea—a love that had grown into the passion for cooking that obsessed me still.

Upon such matters related to food did I reflect as I contemplated the fate of the creatures starving outside my door, a fate to which I had simply been inattentive. Ever since my return, I had been yearning for company to whom I could cater at mealtime, while right outside my door were more prospective dinner guests than I could count.

"I meant what I said," I announced to my animals. "There will be no more food wasted around this household. Every crumb will be eaten from now on. Every crumb. Because whatever we don't eat is going out onto the ground every morning for the birds."

I smiled as I realized that one devious part of my mind was already plotting to dish out more than any of us could eat at each serving—so my conscience would be mollified with the thought that it was only leftovers I was throwing out, after all. I could boil the potato peels, too, and buy day-old bread, clear the freezer and cupboards of things that had been stored for too long, and there were all the cookies left over from Christmas and well, I'd think of more tricks as I went along.

For I would tolerate no more hungry birds around my house. Trash birds or not, pretty birds or not, all were welcome at Margarete's "soup line."

7 Footsteps galloped on the roof, jarring the household tranquillity, as boy squirrel chased girl squirrel for the umpteenth time that day. I smiled, welcoming the sound and its significance. The severe cold had broken, most of the snow was melted, and the animals had begun mating rituals. With its new coat of paint and all the repairs I'd done, the house sparkled and my spirits were bright; winter had been refreshing. Already, I had decided to remain in Falmouth through the summer and was beginning to admit I was going to stay. Despite so many changes, this was still home, something every family needs as a focal point, and I was part of a family.

As I cleared luncheon dishes from the table, Arnie pranced around on Travie's head, parting my grandson's hair with that incessantly busy beak of his, occasionally pausing to tug a lock into a different angle here, to rearrange an unruly strand there. Ignoring his self-appointed hair stylist, Travie knelt on the couch, leaning against its back. His hands were clasped together, his eyes closed, his face upturned.

"Are you praying?" I asked.

"Noooooo."

"What are you doing, then?"

He giggled. "I'm imagining what it will feel like to have snow fall on my face."

Ugh! I had promised him snow when we'd talked on the telephone before he left home. He'd been so excited at the prospect of spending his spring school vacation watching a snowstorm, too. What folly it had been on my part, though, to rely so completely on a weather forecast.

Travie had been glued to the window for three days, and the closest thing to snow he'd seen was a steady, drizzling, icy rain. Florida born and reared, he'd never seen so much as a flake of the real thing and had asked repeatedly what it felt like to be hit by a snowball. It appeared he wasn't going to find out this trip; the sky was beginning to brighten.

"The cartoons should be on now," I said. "Do you want me to turn on the TV set?"

"Uh-uh."

"How about a jigsaw puzzle then. Would you like to help me put together a jigsaw puzzle?"

105

"Uh-uh."

He stared steadily out the window, his chin resting on the backs of folded hands, his fine-featured, freckled face just a few inches from Bundy's broad, hairy one. Arnie lost interest in hair styling, squatted down as though nesting in Travie's hair, and whistled "Mary Had a Little Lamb." I always thought of them as "my three boys" when they were together like that, which was often the case. Sammie and Mitzi loved Travie, too, but there was a special bond linking him and Arnie and Bundy.

"I know," I said, realizing that I was rapidly running out of suggestions for his entertainment. "Why don't you build something with your Lego set? That's one game that Arnie and Bundy always liked to play with you."

He wrinkled his nose and made a face. "I must have made a million-zillion things with the Legos already, Margarete, and it's really work to think of something new. Can't I just look out the window? There's an awful lot to see."

"Well, sure darling, you can look out the window all you want. I just thought you might be bored. What's out there that's so interesting?"

"Lots. You have different kinds of animals here than we do in Florida."

"Oh."

"See, there's Manx!" Travie said excitedly. "Look, he's hanging from the tree and looking right at me!"

Manx was a squirrel, not a cat, but I thought Travie had named him quite appropriately. His tail, though incongruously bushy, was only a bit longer than a nub, and that was only one of countless battle scars Manx sported on his gray coat. While playing hostess to him and his friends during the months since they'd joined my soup line, I'd learned that squirrels are as sweet as cherubs in appearance, some of the most charming creatures on the face of the earth when it comes to begging for a handout, funny as clowns in their antics—and as vicious as fighting cocks when disputing territorial boundaries or the privileges of courtship. A veteran warrior, Manx was king of the neighborhood acorn pile these days, though he seemed to have designated the acorns an emergency reserve since discovering the sunflower seeds and peanut pieces I supplied for the birds.

He swung from the tree branch and sailed about four feet to a landing on the sill outside the window, ran along it until he was in front of Travie, stood tall and straight on his hind legs, and peered into the living room through forepaws braced against the glass. Vagabond reached up a paw and gently placed it on the glass in the middle of Manx's face. The squirrel stretched himself a bit higher so he could see over it and worked his mouth in a chewing motion.

"I think he's ordering dinner, Travie," I said. "Do you want to wait on him today, or shall I?"

"I will, Margarete. Remember, I'm here to help you."

He hadn't reached the ripe age of eight without learning a great deal about chivalry and gentlemanly behavior. In fact, he was being so very solicitous that I'd begun to examine my image in the mirror with some degree of anxiety, looking for a sudden burgeoning of wrinkles or gray hair, telltale signs of frailty, anything that might indicate the sudden galloping advance of old age during the eight months since he's seen me last. No matter how I reassured myself, though, he continued to act as though he thought I might break if I lifted anything heavier than Arnie. Probably just a stage he's going through, I decided optimistically.

"Get the can and dip out some sunflower seeds, Travie," I said. "Remember, though, no more than half a can. I'm trying to wean the little beasties so they'll start looking for their natural foods."

Actually, it was more that I was trying to wean myself from the habits I had developed during the winter. In all honesty, I had to admit that the birds already seemed to be going their own way for food most of the time, seeming to regard my handouts now as extra treats rather than the mainstays they had been a couple of weeks earlier. I didn't find it so easy to move on with the season, however.

Once I had established a spot on my countertop for the bird's scrap dish, once I had begun automatically emptying Arnie's and the cats' and my leftovers into that container, once I had walked a twice-a-day pilgrimage to a specific spot on the lawn to make my offering, it was almost impossible to stop doing so. Now, I would begrudge even a crumb thrown into the garbage, thinking it the magic calorie some bird needed to survive. Besides,

I had to finish making enough room in my freezer so that I could store the summer vegetables for next winter. And while I was caring for the omnivorous birds, I couldn't very well neglect the seed eaters, could I? Or the squirrels. Or Edelweiss and the raccoon I'd chased from my father's bedroom, both of whom had begun making nocturnal appearances again.

I felt responsible for them all. In fact, it had become almost a sacred obligation for me to extend hospitality to the wild animals that frequented my yard, maybe partly because it hit me one day that it had been their yard long before it became mine. I had also come to rely on them for their entertainment value—and for the ego boost it gave me to know they would all miss me, at least for a short while, if anything should happen to me.

I had no idea if my grandson would understand why I fed them, but I was grateful to realize that he found simple joy in the act for his own reasons. "That apple didn't fall far from the tree," is the way my father would have put it. The fact that Travie continued to feel so much for animals even as he grew older and expanded his interests gave me a sense of continuity; like one season following another, my grandson would carry something of my spirit forward into the future long after I had gone.

"Are you okay, Margarete?" The anxiety in Travie's voice snapped me out of my thoughts before they became too morbid. *Better quit looking in the mirror so closely,* I admonished myself.

"I'm just fine, darling," I said.

"It's quit raining. The sun's even coming out. Could we walk to the beach?"

"Oh, well, sure, if you want to. Bundle up real good, though, you hear; it's still pretty cold out there."

"You too," he yelled as he ran to get his coat.

"Me too, what?" I asked when he came back. He had one arm in the jacket, but his contortions made him look like the rubber man in performance at the circus as he struggled to insert the other. I made him stand still and pulled the empty sleeve right side out so he would have a fighting chance in his wrestling match with the jacket.

"Don't help. I can get dressed by myself, you know. You too, bundle up." Triumphantly, he zipped the front of the jacket and reached for his gloves and ski cap. "I don't want you to catch a cold."

Now he was getting just a bit too mature for his britches! Didn't want me to catch a cold, indeed, admonishing me as though he were my parent or nurse or—something! No wonder I was acquiring such a sense of my own mortality lately. I debated whether to ask him why he was having such thoughts of responsibility for my welfare, but decided it was terrible timing for the conversation; he'd been wanting to take this particular walk since the day he'd arrived. What fun was it being so near to the beach if the closest view available was through the window of the car?

"Bye-bye. See you later," Arnie said from his aviary as we opened the front door. "Bye-bye. See

110

you later. Bye-bye."

"Bye-bye, Arnie," Travie replied. "See you later, alligator. He doesn't say that part anymore, does he, Margarete? I haven't heard him say alligator at all since I've been here."

"He's dropped a lot of the things he used to say, Travie, but he's saying a lot of new things instead. I'm not sure if it's because his memory is limited or if he got bored with some of the old words or if he just needs to be reminded constantly about all the ones he knows. I try to remember everything he's ever said and to repeat it to him at least once in a while, but to tell you the truth, I have trouble re-membering all of his words, too. And my brain is much larger than his."

Travie looked up at me with a strange, indeci-pherable expression. "Don't worry, Margarete. I'll be your memory bank." He reached up and patted my arm, then went skipping off up the street, laughing so gleefully that I didn't linger long on his words or the gesture.

Walking was a gait with which he seemed totally unfamiliar; hopping, skipping, jumping, and run-ning were his styles of locomotion. So like his mother at that age, I thought, and so like his grand-mother had been, too. Though he never stopped for an instant, he never went far from me, either, con-stantly coming back to share one observation after another. "The houses sure are built different here . . . This kind of cold air really feels good . . . There was a raccoon in the trees over there, but he ran away . . . Did you know the trees are all waking up after their winter's sleep? . . . How come some days you can see Martha's Vineyard so good and other days you can't see it at all? . . . I'd like to live on an island someday; then I wouldn't have to pay taxes or go to work . . . Sure must be a lot of grubs in the ballpark over there; it's taking a whole flock of Arnies to dig them all up . . . Boy, I sure am glad you don't have condominiums here; they hog all the beach in Florida and don't have any trees around them and they all look like big jails or hospitals . . . Isn't Falmouth nice?"

After he'd skipped stones across the gently lapping waves, tested the water temperature with a tentative forefinger, run along the beach until his shoes were filled with cold sand, and decided that no matter how close the Vineyard looked he'd never be able to throw a rock that far, he was ready for a leisurely walk home. By the time we arrived there, he was happy to curl up in front of the TV set.

"How about a cup of hot chocolate?" I asked. He nodded with enthusiasm, but never took his eyes off the screen, where Mickey Mouse was tiptoeing with a "shushing" forefinger held up before his lips.

Reaching for cups to hold the chocolate, I heard a scream—shrill, penetrating, panic-stricken. I'd heard that particular sound before—twice before, in fact: once when Arnie had become entangled in a string and almost ripped off his foot trying to tear himself free, and once when he'd flown to a landing on the top of a hot pot lid. The scream was repeated three times, then there was silence. Arnie was in trouble!

I dropped the cups, ignoring the shattering sounds as they hit the floor. There was no room in my thoughts for anything except running to Arnie's aid. In four bounding leaps I was out of the kitchen and rounding the corner into the living room. Breathlessly, I looked to the aviary. Within it, Arnie sat on the middle perch, nonchalantly looking about with total unconcern.

"You scared the wits out of me, Arnie," I said as I walked up and peered in at him.

He hopped down one perch, said, "Gimme a kiss," and made smacking noises as he touched his beak to the screening in front of my lips.

"Nothing wrong with you, is there. Don't you dare screech like that again unless you're in real trouble. Did I ever tell you the story about the little shepherd boy who cried 'Wolf' so often that no one helped him when the real wolf did show up? You—"

EAEAEEEeeeeeeeeeeeeeeeeeeeeeeeEEEAEHHH! Eeeeeeeeee. Eeeeeeh.

Arnie's neck stretched a good three inches as he stood tall and looked around, his head swiveling in a careful arc from right to left before he froze, with his beak pointing toward the front door. No doubt about it, the scream had come from outside the house, in the yard. It was a starling distress call.

"Sorry about the scolding, Arnie," I said as I hurried to the window and looked out. There were no signs of a bird in distress. I opened the door and checked from that perspective. Still nothing. Shrugging, I closed the door and leaned against it, frowning. Though I'd seen nothing out of the ordinary, there was something that simply felt not right out there. I listened for the scream to sound again; perhaps I could locate it if I heard it again—if I heard— of course! That's what was wrong—I hadn't seen a thing through the window, and I hadn't heard a sound when I'd opened the door. It was so still, so silent, that it seemed every living creature had suddenly vacated the neighborhood.

EEEEeeeeeeeeeeeee!

The cause of that shrill, desperate screech was undoubtedly the reason every living creature had vacated the neighborhood! This time, I had it pinpointed for sure. I ran to my bedroom window and froze in my tracks.

On the ground, in front of the woodpile and not more than three feet away from the house, was a light gray bird, as still as death. All I could see in that first instant was its shoulders and the bow of its neck, and they were obscure within the shadow cast by the tree beneath which I usually fed the birds. A mourning dove? A very large mourning dove? Uttering starling distress calls? How little I still knew about the birds! My grossly mistaken impression lasted for only the few seconds it took him to lift his head majestically and look at me with imperious disdain. His amber eyes fixed upon me from behind the hooked beak of a predator. He was magnificent! And he was much too busy at his calling to be concerned with a mere human who didn't even know a gentle dove from a bird of prey.

Lying on its back, completely imprisoned by the

hawk's strong talons, its belly vulnerable and exposed to that efficient beak, was a starling. It could easily have passed for Arnie. Even the expression on its face, a glare of defiance rather than a grimace of fear, would have been Arnie's typical reaction. Leisurely, as though it had all the time in the world, the hawk reached down nuzzled the starling's chest with a gesture of apparent loving gentleness, then came up with a beak full of feathers. The starling didn't twitch a muscle. The hawk arched its neck, opened its beak, and stretched toward the smaller bird's chest once again.

"Nooo!" I cried through two layers of window glass. "No you don't, you beast. Get away from here. Go away. This isn't your territory. Go away! Don't you touch one more feather, you hear me. Go away, I tell you!"

Slowly, ever so slowly, the hawk lifted its head, swiveled its beak to point in my direction, and fixed me with a glare so fierce that I froze and quit my frenzied pounding on the window. Those eyes locked onto mine. My breath stopped in my throat. For a tick of time frozen in eternity, its very essence bored into me. The effect was so mesmerizing that

115

I understood, I knew, I felt to the depth of my being why the starling was not resisting. It couldn't. The hawk nuzzled it again. Abruptly, the starling's head slumped to the side and it looked toward me. Its eyes gleamed, then glazed over.

With a knot in my throat so large I thought I would choke, I banged on the window glass again. The hawk unfurled its wings, gave me a final look of contempt, and took to the air, carrying its dinner with effortless grace. The starling's head flopped limply from a body embraced tightly within those terrible talons.

I watched until the hawk disappeared from sight beyond the trees, realizing as I did so how foolishly impractical my reaction had been. After all, the hawk had to eat, too, and nature dictated that he do exactly as he had done. Even so, the prey he had chosen had looked so much like Arnie, and in a way it, too, had been my starling. How dare the hawk make a meal of one of my starlings?

With a sigh and a shrug at my helplessness to change the natural order of things, I turned away from the window. And bumped into Travie, who was standing right at my elbow. Seeing the look of horror on his face, I didn't have to ask how much he had seen. Great tears coursed down his cheeks.

I put my arm around his shoulders, squeezed his biceps, and led him to the kitchen table. I started to sweep up the broken cup fragments, but he took the broom from my grasp with great solemnity and did the job for me. His eyes were downcast the whole time; he didn't utter a sound. When he looked up, his tears were dried into telltale tracks streaking his face. He'd never been a crying kid, but he had the good sense to be unashamed of having done it.

I poured hot chocolate into the two fresh cups I'd put on the table, dropped some marshmallows into his, and put a plateful of chocolate chip cookies between us. He bit into a cookie and sipped at the beverage without much enthusiasm.

"It hurt me, too," I said. "Some people feel better when they keep things inside of themselves; some people feel better when they talk about what hurts. I'm a talker myself. How about you?"

He shrugged, sipped, nibbled at the cookie. One tear trickled down to the corner of his mouth and hung there. He flicked it off with the tip of his tongue. "I thought it was our Arnie for a minute."

"It felt that way to me, too, for a while."

"I've seen dead things before," he said slowly, "but I never saw anything die. I mean, one minute the Arnie was looking at me, then all of a sudden he wasn't a he anymore; he was just a dead . . . thing."

"That's what death is, you know. No matter how it happens, death is just a matter of the life force leaving the body. Without the life force, a body is just a thing."

"Is Arnie going to die someday?"

"Yes, but not for a long, long time, I hope. No hawks are going to get to him in here. He should live for about fifteen years, maybe even longer if we're lucky. You'll be a grown man by then."

He was quiet for a long while. Sipping chocolate and nibbling a cookie, he stared at the tabletop, avoiding my eyes. I had to bite my tongue, to force myself to wait for him to ask the question in his own words, in his own time. In a way, I wished he would have asked it of his mother instead of me. I was feeling about as tough as an egg at the moment.

"When are you going to die, Margarete?" he said at last.

The words were like a kick in the stomach. I'd been prepared for "Are you . . . ?" Not for "When . . . ?" So I laughed. "I haven't the slightest idea, darling."

"It's not funny," he said grumpily. Then his words came out in a torrent. "My friend's grandmother was always laughing and happy and having a good time with him. Then, one day, she got sick and went to the hospital, and they wouldn't let him in to see her. They just told him she died one night. He had to go to a funeral and look inside a coffin, but he said it wasn't her in there, it was just a body. He still can't get over that he never got to see her again. And that's what I'm afraid you're going to do to me. Someday I'll go home to Florida and then one day Mom will tell me you died and I'll just never, ever see you again. It's not fair!"

It was my turn to sip chocolate and nibble on a cookie and be quiet. I lit a cigarette, too. And stared out the window.

"Well?" he said.

"Well, what?"

"Well, aren't you going to say it won't be that way?"

"I've never lied to you before, Travie, and I'm not going to start now. I don't think it's fair, either, but that's probably exactly what will happen. All I can say is that I'll live as long as I can. And I promise you, if I ever get so sick that I think I'll die, I'll send for you so you can see me one last time, hospital rules or no hospital rules. I understand exactly how you feel."

"You do?"

"Of course. I know how I'd feel if you, oh, said you were going to the beach, but instead of coming back here you went home to Florida without saying good-bye to me. You see, I'll bet the part that hurt your friend the most was that he didn't get to say good-bye to his grandmother before she left him. Maybe he had a few other special things he would have liked to tell her if he'd known it was going to be his last chance to see her."

"Yeah, I guess you're right, Margarete."

"I'll tell you what we can do. We can say our final good-byes now, and then we won't have to worry about whether or not we'll have the chance later on."

"Huh?"

"Let's pretend. Let's pretend that I'm going to live forever, but I'm going to have to move to another planet to do it. Of course, that means you and I will never, ever see or hear from each other again. Naturally, you'll come to the spaceport to say good-bye to me, won't you?"

119

"Sure."

"Okay. I'm going to the departure gate in the other room to wait for you. And you pretend you just came in on the space shuttle from the moon. Then I want you to do and say whatever you would want to the very last time we ever, ever see each other." I walked into the living room and stared through the window.

"Grandmother, grandmother," he said and threw his arms around my waist. "Don't go away and leave me."

"You've always called me Margarete; don't stop now. Travie, you know that no one can live on earth forever. You know I have to leave you no matter how much I want to stay. As long as you love me, though, a part of me will always be with you. Having you for my grandson has been one of the best parts of my whole life. I'm so glad I was able to stay around long enough to watch you grow up and become a professional jet jockey."

He giggled but continued with his role. "And I'm so glad I had you for a grandmother. I love you, Margarete, so I guess you will always be with me. Do you have to take Arnie and Bundy and Sammie and Mitzi with you, though? They won't like Pluto." He giggled again, though a bit nervously.

"You're right, Travie, they can't go with me. So I've decided to leave them all with you. You will take good care of them and love them, won't you?"

"Sure!"

"Well, I guess that's it, then. Good-bye, Travie. I love you. Thanks for being my grandson."

"And I love you, Margarete. Good-bye. Thanks for being my grandmother."

We hugged. Very tightly. His eyes glistened suspiciously as I walked out the front door.

I strolled around the block before going back into the house. He was sitting in my chair watching television when I opened the door. Bundy was on one side of him, Sammie on the other, and Arnie perched on his head. He lifted Bundy to the arm of the chair, put Sammie into his lap, moved way over to one side of the chair, and patted the cushion next to him. I sat and put my arm around his shoulders.

"Feel better?" I asked.

He lifted up, gave me a long kiss on the cheek, and said, "Uh-huh."

"You realize, of course, that I fully intend to be around for another twenty or thirty years or more. I have to finish watching you grow up. And I have to teach your children all about loving animals. By the time we really have to say good-bye, we might think of a few more things we want to say."

"Uh-uh," he said adamantly. "We've said it all."

8 Another man came into my life that year, a young one. He was charming, handsome, witty, kind, fun to be with, and just a tad lost, as are most fifteen-year-olds.

David had it a bit tougher than many of his peers, however. His mother, afflicted with poor health, was frequently in and out of the hospital. The family had learned to cope over the years, and Chrissie always pulled the weight of homemaker in Martha's absence; but now that my niece was grown, she also had job responsibilities. With Linda away at college, David often went home to an empty house these days.

Realizing that, I'd felt really needed when Martha was hospitalized again and asked me to pick up my nephew after school each day. Aunt Margarete, charging to the rescue in her blue-and-white Blazer, that was me—and reveling in the role. I'd always wanted a son, preferably a big brother for my daughter, but Hanna had been my first and only child. A nephew, though, was almost as close a substitute son as a grandchild, and David lived right in the same town with me, so I could see him often.

Strictly as an aunt, though. My brother's family was a tight one with open lines of communication and a lot of love within it. So David was as strong and secure as they come at that age, with no need of my mothering. As it turned out, it was he who had come to my rescue. Without his help, I don't think I could have managed all the outdoor cleanup and repair that faced me that spring. Watching him work, his entire concentration bent to the task, I speculated on what a fine man he was going to be, though I seriously doubted if he'd ever be able to earn a living as a carpenter.

He tapped the big twelve-penny nail as though it might rise up and strike him back if he hit it too hard. Knowing the fragility of teenage egos, I refrained from telling him he was doing it all wrong. Instead, I turned to the task of hammering together my section of the fence framework. I would do it so efficiently that he would learn from my example. Perhaps he would even be so impressed with his aunt's ability that he would ask me to teach him the proper way to drive home such large nails. Over the months, I'd grown fond of this nephew I'd never known, and I wasn't above wanting to show off my expertise just a bit.

Tap, tap, tap, tap, tap, tap sounded David's hammer to every *Ka-wham!* blow of my own. Any second, my nail would sink into the wood all the way to its head while David's would overheat and twist into some impossible angle, I thought smugly. *Tap, tap, tap, twomp!* Our happy harmony ended in mid-beat as David's nail bent, exactly as I had known it would. I bit my lip to keep it from curling into a smile and lifted my hammer for another mighty blow. *Ka-schonk!* It rang dully as my target bent to an even more impossible angle than David's had.

"Guess this is going to take a while, Aunt Margarete," he said. "But don't worry, I can build the fence for you if you'd rather tackle something easier."

I was having too much fun with him to go off and do something separately. As we labored, he cracked jokes, told me little anecdotes about his school and friends and family, and genuinely seemed to enjoy the time we were spending together. He could have been playing street hockey or basketball or video games with friends, but he had volunteered to help me instead. "I have to be nice while I can," he'd explained. "I'm going to be a Boston Bruin someday, so pretty soon I have to start learning about being mean." I was certain that he'd never have a mean bone in his body, of course, though I'd already seen him in action with his youth team and knew that he was really a good hockey player. I assured him that skill, not meanness, was what he'd need to keep working on if he wanted to be good at the adult version of the game. He'd looked at me as though pitying me for my naiveté, but was too polite to contradict his aunt.

"Er, thanks, David, but we'll do it together. I'm happy that you're helping me, but I wouldn't want to overwork you."

He glanced up from the bent nail he was prying out of the wood and gestured with his head toward the house. "If you don't plan to overwork me," he said, "would you please tell your foreman to quit giving me such dirty looks."

The "foreman" sat on the nearest window sill, her nose pressed against the screen, her fat face frowning with impatience. Mitzi was the reason the fence was the top priority item on my repair list. She'd spent most of the winter on the fireplace hearth, contentedly purring in a state bordering on hibernation. Now, though, she was too restless to sleep at all, and so anxious to be outside that I felt like a terrible troll holding her free spirit imprisoned.

I blamed her newfound discontent on Manx, who teased her unmercifully. When Mitzi lay sunning herself upon a window sill, he made good use of his acrobatic skills to hang by his toes from the shutter so he could bang the screen in front of her face. When she was at the door, looking out, that mischief-making squirrel would charge across the lawn and up the porch steps, take a flying leap that landed him in a belly-flop across the glass of the storm door, and look back over his shoulder at her as he sauntered away with a waggle of his hind quarters. I couldn't help thinking that he was telling her to come out and play.

But that was something I would not permit until I had catproofed the entire fence line surrounding the back yard. The measure was for my own protection, of course: pets that wander all too often have shortened life spans and owners with prematurely gray hair. There would be no wanderers from my household. With any small degree of skill, David and I could finish ensuring that fact within the hour. Given our propensity for bending nails instead of sinking them properly, however, I was afraid it might take us a wee bit of a day or two longer. By sunset we did manage to have the fence frame standing upright, its support posts fitted into holes in the ground, and those filled with wet concrete.

"Well," I said, "looks like we've done all we can for today."

"No, we haven't," he said. "Now we have to do the most important part." He picked up a nail and looked at me quizzically. "What's Travie's middle initial?"

"It's R—for Raymond, his father's name."

"Oh. My middle name is the same as Dad's, too. Guess that's to make sure they don't forget we're their sons." He bent to the wet concrete and began to scratch with the nail. "I can't just leave it unmarked. This fence will be our monument. Someday the archaeologists will find it, and people will think we were somebody special."

"By tomorrow, you'll already be somebody special, at least as far as Mitzi is concerned. If she kept memoirs, she'd make a notation that the week this fence was built was one of the best in her life."

The next day was Saturday, and David had been assigned to check out the family beach cabin for winter storm damage, but he stopped by my house first to assure me that he'd return to help me later. As he rode off on his bicycle, I reached for the hammer and a fencing board, humming with simple joie de vivre.

What a spring it was! If awards were given to the seasons, this one would certainly take the prize. Each day the sky was a rich, velvety blue with just enough wispy white clouds to adorn it like tasteful touches of lace. Though the nights were cold and an occasional chunk of ice still floated in the ocean, the days were warm and filled with the promise of summer. Crocuses were fading as daffodils and tulips took their turn at proclaiming the season. Forsythia bushes, ablaze with yellow blossoms, were downright ostentatious in contrast to the last, clinging dinginess of winter. Rhododendron and azalea buds had fattened to their utmost and were simply awaiting their turn to burst open and spray the world with vivid hues. And the color green, in all its varied shades, was being reborn to the landscape.

All that vibrancy of life reawakening, combined with the crisp salt tanginess of Cape Cod air, was enough to make me want to climb mountains and sing operettas and run the Boston Marathon all at

the same time. I settled for humming and hammering.

Resounding clearly from inside the house, Arnie's voice joined mine with snatches of Beethoven's
Fifth Symphony, "Mary Had a Little Lamb," and
an assortment of very human whistles combined
into his own unique tunes. Even his vocabulary
took on an especially melodious quality as he har-
monized with the rhythmic rapping of my hammer.
I wondered if he was as happy as he sounded,
cooped up indoors as he was. Sunshine and fresh
air and the stimulation of watching nature's normal
activities would be good for him, I was certain. This
year, he was going to get daily outings while I
worked in the yard, just as the cats would.

And, if I didn't let Mitzi join me soon, one of the
two of us was going to have a nervous breakdown.

She danced over when I sat down to lunch,
jumped onto my lap, put her front paws on my
shoulders, and licked my face. "What *are* you
doing, Mip-Mip?" I asked. "You've never kissed
me in your life!" She did it again, her tongue tic-
kling my cheek with its roughness. Arnie stopped
prancing on the table, stood stock still, and
stared at her. "You're going insane!" I said. She
meowed and nuzzled my chin with hers. Arnie
reached out, grabbed her tail, and gave it a good
tweak. She looked at him, snorted, jumped to
the floor, and positioned herself at the door.
"Meeeeooooowwww?" she said, looking yearningly
at me.

Manx bounced up the porch steps, put his paws

against the storm door, and peered inside. Mitzi pressed her face to the glass so that they were nose to nose, my cat and that troublesome squirrel, making cow eyes at each other like two lovers.

"That is completely unnatural behavior," I told them between bites of sandwich. "I hope you have the good sense to keep your distance when she goes out, Manx. She is a cat, you know."

"Coo-coo, peek-a-boo, Mitzi loves the boo," Arnie said. "Kissy, kissy, bye-bye."

"Maybe Mitzi loves the boo, but if she goes kissy, kissy, it really could mean bye-bye for Manx. Never trust a cat's friendship all the way, Arnie, never."

I took another bite of my sandwich while Arnie picked at the lettuce that had fallen onto my plate. As I chewed, Mitzi and Manx stared at me, and stared, and stared. "Look, Mip-Mip," I said at last. "I can't hang the gate until David comes back to help me. I'm going to take a chance and let you come out with me after lunch, though. But if you go anywhere near the opening in the fence, you'll be back inside so fast your head will spin."

Finished with lunch, I carried my dishes back to the sink and gave them a quick wash. Arnie tip-tapped nervously on the countertop, ruffling his feathers and giving hasty nudges to his wings and feathers. "You want a bath, right, little duck?" I said. He shook his feathers so vigorously that his feet slid around on the slick Formica. Standing patiently in his margarine-bowl bathtub, he watched it fill with tepid tap water. I held a dishtowel like a shower curtain in front of the sink and braced for

the splashes. "Good! *Pweet, pweet, pweet, pweet, pweet, pweet, pweet* . . . Arnie-ly. I love . . . good, good." He sang as his wings flung water onto his back and over the towel into my face and onto the floor.

"Aunt Margarete, there's a storm in your sink!" David said over my shoulder.

"Just a little April shower," I said. "Won't last long. Hi. How did you find the beach house?"

"Occupied." His voice cracked.

His tone made me turn around and look. Cradled in the palms of his hands was a bird's nest, within which were nestled three teeny-tiny naked hatchlings, their eyes still glued shut.

Arnie jumped from the sink to the counter, gave himself one good shake, and flew toward the living room. "Be with you in a minute," I said and followed my bird to his cage. Closing his door, I locked it, left him to his preening, and returned to David.

"There was a broken window," he said, looking at his charges with a shine in his eyes. "Their parents were inside, on the floor. Something had torn them to shreds. These guys were screaming bloody murder up on a rafter."

I touched each bird in turn. They were cold as ice. One stirred a bit; another jerked its head up, opened its mouth wide and peeped feebly; the other was already dead. When the live ones breathed, they wheezed. "Let's get them into the guest room," I said. "It's warmer in there, and I don't want to take a chance that Arnie might catch a disease from them."

While David cupped his hand over them as I'd instructed, warming them with his own body heat, I turned on the electric blanket that had been on the twin bed since Travie's visit and whipped back the covers. Removing the dead bird, I wrapped him in a paper towel and put it on top of the freezer. I transferred his siblings to a makeshift nest of soft tissue paper that David had tucked into a plastic bowl, put that into a large cardboard box in the middle of the bed, and covered it all with the sheet, warmed blanket, and a down comforter.

"Won't they suffocate?" David said.

"No. There's enough air in that box to last them days. Let's see if we can get food into them. Could you tell what kind of birds the parents were?"

"Purple finches, I think."

"Seed eaters. Well, we don't have time to be choosy. I guess any kind of protein will do." I mixed some peanut butter with cat food and just

131

enough water so I could draw it into an eyedropper, sprinkled in a bit of the antibiotic that had once saved Arnie's life, and carried it to the guest room.

"Will they make it?" David asked anxiously.

"Maybe this one will," I said as I doled food into the throat of the bird with the open mouth. "This one's just about gone," I said of the hatchling that responded to my finger taps with only feeble twitches. With nothing to lose, I gripped the corners of its wide mouth between my thumb and forefinger, pulled gently until its neck was extended and beak opened, and placed a glob at the back of its tongue. With obvious effort, it swallowed. "Never force food that they can't swallow," I counseled as I worked. "It would get into the airways and strangle them." Drop after drop I globbed until its crop bulged at the neck and it would swallow no more. Then I returned to the gaping baby until it, too, quit swallowing; its head collapsed with wobbly motions onto its brother's back and both slept.

"Tough little guys," David said, wiping at his eyes with a tissue. "You're really some nurse, Aunt Margarete," he said, blowing his nose.

"Only nurse enough to see that your allergy's acting up." I said as I pulled the covers back over the box. "Let's get outside to the fresh air. Sleep's the only thing that can help them now." I picked up the tiny bundle from the freezer, closed the bedroom door behind us, and put my hand on David's shoulder as we walked through the house.

"Hi there," Arnie said when he saw us. "Hello. Did you come see me? C'mere, kiss Arnie."

David detoured to the aviary. "Hi there, Arnie," he said. "Was he that tiny when you found him, Aunt Margarete? Was he as bad off as they are?"

"He was larger. Finches are much smaller than starlings at every stage. Birds don't have as many years to grow as humans, so they're hatched pretty close to the size they'll be as adults, then feathers make them appear much larger than they really are. Arnie was a pretty pitiful specimen, though, and it was days before I decided that he might survive."

"Then there's hope for them, too?"

"Where there's life, there's always hope, David."

"Will you get them over the hump? Please? Then I'll take over until they're ready to fly."

"I'll do my best, but don't count too much on their making it. They already have a respiratory problem, I'm afraid. Baby birds are some of the most fragile creatures on the face of the earth, and humans really can't cope with their needs very well. At best, I'll fumble my way through the feedings, and, if they're lucky, I won't wind up killing them by accident. If you hadn't found them when you did, though, they wouldn't have had even the small chance of survival that we're going to give them."

He laughed without humor. "Funny. Somehow I feel as though I've just become the father of premature babies."

"Then it's a good time for you to learn that keeping himself occupied is the most useful thing a father can do when a baby needs sleep. We'll feed them every fifteen minutes or so at first, but meanwhile we'll be nervous wrecks if we don't keep busy.

Let's go to work."

"Let's go to work," Arnie repeated.

"Smart aleck starling. You're one boss too many around here," David told him. "Where's the shovel, Aunt Margarete?"

He took the enshrouded baby bird from my hands and put it into the original nest, burying them together in my backyard. When the second hatchling died less than two hours later, he re-opened the hole and laid it beside its brother. The third one put up a valiant struggle, but the wheezing got ever worse and it went steadily downhill as the sun descended in the sky. By late afternoon, it too, was gone, and the three siblings rested together in the ground.

I let Mitzi out when we sat on the back porch to rest and contemplate the little mound of disturbed dirt. She moved warily about on the patio, chewing blades of grass and sniffing at every centimeter of ground. To my relief, Manx had disappeared, probably because I hadn't thrown out sunflower seeds on demand. He didn't fool me one bit—he came to the doors and windows for handouts, not friendship. I certainly hoped Mitzi could see through him, too. I wouldn't want her heart broken by a mangy squirrel.

"I'm sorry I went to the cabin today." David said, blowing his nose. "Darn allergy. If I'd waited until tomorrow, you wouldn't have had all that trouble for nothing, Aunt Margarete."

"It wasn't for nothing, David. You learned a lot today. Maybe someday that knowledge will come in handy. Maybe the next baby bird you find will make it, or the one after that. All of life is about trying. Everything is chancy, but nothing at all gets accomplished without trying. Don't you ever forget that, either. Never refuse to try just because things don't always work out."

I lit a cigarette and smoked in silence as we watched Mitzi run to an oak tree. She scraped the bark over and over, sharpening the claws her cotton paws didn't have. Suddenly she was off and running across the yard. Each step was a long leap as she pounced with her front legs, then kicked her heels high into the air in the most joyful gait I'd ever seen. She stopped for a moment at another tree, sniffed up and down and around the trunk, and scraped its bark. Abruptly, she stopped, looked around the tree toward April's yard, flattened her ears against her head, and took off running like a streak of lightning.

"Mitzi!" I yelled as she neared the fence. "Mitzi, don't you dare!" She had always been a mighty leaper whenever it suited her fancy to indulge in athletics. With the momentum she was building up, I knew she'd have no trouble clearing that fence. "No, Mitzi!" I had nightmare visions of her running into the path of a speeding car, of her being beaten to shreds by an aggressive tomcat, of her being kidnaped, of me roaming the neighborhood in the dead of the night, still searching for her. "Pleeeaaase, Mitzi, stop."

She did. Right at the fence line. And started to wash her face as nonchalantly as though cleanliness had been the topmost thought on her mind during the entire spurting run.

Panting for breath by the time I arrived at her side, I looked down into the most innocent expression imaginable. When I put my hands on my hips, debating in my mind whether to make her go back inside or not, she turned her gaze from me and looked through the fence as though I wasn't even there. "Well, Mip-Mip, either I have to learn to trust you or we'll both be unhappy while I keep you imprisoned for life." She ambled off to sniff at the base of the nearest bush.

I allowed her to continue her explorations until David and I had finished with the gate and checked over the rest of the fence for possible escape routes for the black cats. Tomorrow would be their day. I was certain now that I wouldn't have cause to worry about Mitzi. Finished exploring, she seemed quite content with the one spot in the fence line to which she had first run.

"You know, Aunt Margarete," David said, "I was just a little kid then, but I could swear I remember Mitzi sitting in that same spot day in and day out when Grandma and Grandpa Sigl were alive."

"Why, of course, you're right, David! I had completely forgotten until you mentioned it. We always called it Mitzi's mole hole. The entrance to a mole family's burrow was there. She used to sit in that same spot for hours and days and weeks on end, waiting for one of them to poke its nose up. Then she'd chase it, of course."

"Did she ever catch them?"

"Once in a great while she would. Then she'd bring it to me or one of your grandparents as if it was a gift she was very proud of giving to us."

"Were they dead or alive?"

"Alive. She carried them exactly the way she would a kitten. The poor things were terrified, but otherwise unharmed."

"You mean she didn't even hurt them?"

"Well, just once. She dropped one before presenting it properly, and it ran straight at me. I suspect Mitzi thought it was attacking me because she grabbed it, gave a quick twitch of her head, and broke its neck as cleanly as an expert. That made me realize that her instincts are quite intact. She'd have no trouble hunting for her meals if she had to, though I can't imagine how she'd manage to get them cleaned, cooked, and minced to suit her finicky tastes."

"Cats can be . . . well, vicious, can't they? I'll bet it was a cat that killed the finches in our beach cabin."

"Probably was. Cats are predators by nature. They can be taught, though, with a great deal of patience. Between my father and me, we broke Mitzi of chasing birds. Even so, I usually don't let her out without a good loud bell on her collar."

"What about Samantha and Vagabond? Would they hurt your birds?"

"They'd better not even try! Though I admit it'll be up to me to see to it that they don't."

"Then you're going to let them out, too?"

"Sure, why not?" The answer to that question wouldn't be bursting my bubble of happiness for a while yet.

9 Mitzi bounded outside like a gamboling colt, frisked as far as the edge of the patio, then dropped to her belly. Her ears flattened against her head, her tail swished, her rear end wiggled, and she was off and running with the no-nonsense speed and posture of a cat serious about catching prey—with Manx as the intended prey. Intent on the acorn he was munching in the middle of the yard, he'd never even see her coming! I opened my mouth and shouted a warning. He looked up, dropped his acorn, and bounced across the ground—straight toward Mitzi. She stopped. He stopped. She leaned her head first to one side, then the other, looking at him. He took two steps forward, four steps backward, six steps forward, and danced a little jig in front of her.

Then the chase was on. Round and round the tree they ran, Mitzi never more than two inches away from Manx's stub of a tail—though she never seemed to get an iota closer than that two inches, either, no matter how often Manx glanced backward over his shoulder. Suddenly he came to a screeching halt, stood, turned around, and looked up at her. She braked, sat, and looked down at him, her mouth open and panting from the unaccustomed exertion.

The prey waited for the predator to catch her breath, then took two steps toward her, four steps back, six steps forward, and repeated his dancing jig while she wiggled her hind end and crouched in the classic posture of a cat readying for the spring. Manx bounced and Mitzi pounced, and they were off and running again, zigging and zagging, crissing and crossing and circling, spurting and slowing, leaping and lunging with such synchronous movements that it could have been an energetic ballet they'd carefully choreographed long before the moment arrived for the actual performance.

When he became bored with the game, Manx ran up an oak, stood on a lower branch long enough to wave his tail in farewell, then lunged to an overhanging limb of the neighbor's hickory tree and sailed from branch to branch on his way to other parts of town. Mitzi stood upright against the base of the tree where they'd parted company, watched him until he'd disappeared from sight, cleaned her paws on the bark, and pranced to the patio with the expression of Alice's Cheshire. She lay down next to my chair and licked my hand.

"Do you feel better now?" I asked. "As I remember it, you used to chase all of the squirrels exactly the way you chased Manx. Funny how they seem to know you'd never harm them."

Behind us, Bundy meowed long and plaintively. I looked over my shoulder and saw him and Sammie with their noses and front paws pressed to the door glass. Mitzi glared at them, hissed, growled, and walked off to explore the hedges at the back of the yard.

I went back into the house and picked up Arnie in his travel cage from the kitchen table. "Okay, gang, I promised all of you a play day and this is it." I held the door open for the black cats. "Well, are you two going to stand there all day? I thought you wanted to go outside." Sammie looked at the opening to the world, turned, and started to slink toward the living room. I scooped her up and tucked her under my free arm. Bundy froze in place halfway through the door, realizing that this time I wasn't going to stop his usual sneaky dash toward freedom. Arnie looked out with only mild curiosity.

"Love your enthusiasm, gang," I said. "C'mon, get with it. You're going to have fun whether you want to or not."

I put the side of my foot against the tail tucked between Bundy's legs and gave him a little shove. He hissed, crouched with his belly about a centimeter off the concrete porch, and undulated to the ground like a centipede on the way to its own execution. Sammie struggled as though I might throw her into a tub of water when I walked through the door. Arnie flew straight up, banged his head on the top of the cage, then tried to lunge his way through the screening of the sides and door. I sighed, put the cage on the patio table, and lowered Sammie to the ground. She ran over to her son and licked his face furiously. He growled and hugged the ground even tighter. Arnie crouched on his topmost perch and trembled.

"The three of you are being ridiculous," I said. "Look at Mitzi. She's having a wonderful time." At the mole hole, she stared through the fence with an intensity that reminded me of a cow yearning for the greener grass.

A car backfired. Arnie fell forward, struggled for balance, and wound up dangling upside down from his perch. Bundy scuttled back onto the porch. Looking up, he meowed at the door as though ordering it to open for him. Sammie made a beeline for the farthest corner of the yard, scaled the wire fencing, and was out of sight before Arnie regained his feet. "So much for the great outdoors." I said. I trudged up the porch steps with Arnie and opened the door. Bundy crawled inside and wedged himself under my easy chair. Arnie flew to a lamp, flapped his wings mightily, and screeched a starling scold before retiring to the aviary. I brought Mitzi in and went in search of Samantha.

Four hours later I was still searching, still calling and growing progressively more hoarse and grouchy. It was a beautiful day, practically a summer day, and there were a thousand things I'd rather be doing, not to mention another two thousand things I should be doing. For the dozenth time, I rounded the hedges from my yard and started to walk up the property line of April's yard.

She was sitting in a lawn chair on her patio. "Aha!" I said. "I caught you playing hooky." I had to force the joviality, just as I'd had to struggle for words each time I'd seen April lately. The inanity of the things that tumbled out of my mouth always embarrassed me as soon as they'd been spoken. I'm no good at coping with another person's pain.

Christine had broken the news to me weeks ago. I'd listened in stunned disbelief to her words over the telephone, "Aunt Margarete, did you hear? April's son died last night."

"Ricky? What happened? An accident?"

"I don't know," Chrissie said. "I just heard about it myself and thought you'd want to know."

I hung up the phone and looked through the curtains. Lights burned on both porches and in every room of April's house; cars lined her driveway and both sides of the street. I'd neither heard nor noticed their arrival. I picked up the phone and called Ray and Claire, the neighbors on the other side of me, and broke the news to them. Then I informed Ruth across the street. "With all those people consoling her, I'd probably just be in the way if I went over," I said to myself. There'd be relatives from out of town, friends from far and near, I knew, because April has always drawn friends like a magnet, people who truly love her for the dear person she is. I hadn't seen enough of her since I'd been back to regard myself as an intimate, but I wanted to do something more concrete than mumble hollow words of condolence. Chewing on a nail, staring through the window, I pondered what to do. "With all those people consoling her, she has a mob to feed. I'll whip up something for them to eat," I decided.

I went to the freezer and took out all the ground beef I could find. Not fancy fare, but it would be quick and worry free when her company was hungry. Getting out my largest pots, I started a nameless dish of macaroni, stewed tomatoes, and beef that I'd discovered in Texas.

"I cannot believe it," I muttered as I cooked. It seemed as though fate had dictated parallel tragedies for Patsy and April. Both of them had been widowed prematurely and left to raise their children alone. Now they'd lost sons within a year of each other. Even the boys' names were the same, though spelled differently—Patsy's Riki, April's Ricky. Stunned, I could only stir the tomatoes, shake my head, and sputter. "Why, I just saw Ricky over the holidays! We were talking about the way he and Nancy used to talk to my father through the fence, understanding everything he said despite Papa's gosh-awful broken English. And about how they'd knocked on the door every day for some of Mama's cookies. Those kids really meant a lot to my parents. They'd be so sad about Ricky."

Chopping onions, garlic, and peppers, I let the

tears stream down my cheeks as I reminisced about the days when Hanna had felt herself a big sister and my parents had regarded themselves as great-aunt and uncle to the kids next door. Their father—an accountant, a soft-spoken, kind, tall man—had been alive then. Elliott cherished his family, who'd been devastated when he died so young of a heart attack. Like Patsy, April had proved to be a strong woman when widowed, taking charge and simultaneously working to support her children while nurturing them with all the love in the world. Would she also be strong enough to survive this additional blow?

The loss of a child is the most awful grief any human being can be forced to endure. I had a friend who'd been unable to quit crying for years after her son passed away. And another who'd developed selective amnesia, blocking out all memory of a daughter who'd died. I understood how they felt, too.

There had been a time, an eternally long night of terror, when I'd thought my daughter was lost to me. We'd had a terrible quarrel over a young man she was dating. I had forbidden her to go out with him, but I was working in Boston at the time and she was on the Cape, already old enough to be making her own rules had she been independent of me. I'd known even while we were shouting that there was no way I could enforce my orders, that we had finally come to that parting of the ways when child judges parent and decides whether rebellion is necessary to end the rule of the benevolent dictator.

Late that night, while listening to the radio, I heard a news report about a fatal accident on the Cape that had claimed the life of a young man and an unidentified companion who would not be named until next of kin had been notified. The one victim named was the young man over whom Hanna and I had quarreled—and no one answered the telephone when I called home. I assumed the worst, jumped into my car, and rushed home. As it turned out, Hanna had cried herself into a sound sleep after telling the young man she wouldn't be going out with him that night, and hadn't heard the telephone ring when I called. But before I knew she was safe, I died a thousand agonizing times myself, thinking that my daughter was the "unidentified companion" who'd been killed in that accident. Aside from the pain, I'd felt only overwhelming anger at the fates for taking away my child so prematurely.

If I were April now, I'd be enraged. When I'd returned home, she'd been elated that a new surgical technique had cured Ricky of the same congenital heart defect that had killed his father and haunted his own childhood. For the first time in years, April was free of concern. Nancy had grown into a pretty, witty young lady and was attending college. Ricky, the spitting image of his attractive father, was charming, bright, healthy, and on his way to fulfilling his lifelong ambition. He'd graduated from college and found a job in Boston—strictly something to pay the bills while he struggled to become acknowledged as a writer. A tragic tale with a finally happy ending their lives had seemed.

And now Ricky was dead. He'd been—what?—twenty-two or three? Maybe a bit older. Certainly too young for his life to be over. But then, everyone is too young to die who hasn't finished living life to its fullest. That's why I'd like to be convinced of reincarnation, a cycle of living over and over again until we're all fulfilled in our mortal existences. How wonderfully sensible and just that seems. Oh, how I'd like to be convinced it's so.

Dark philosophy, tears, and remembrances went into my biggest soup pot right along with the more substantial ingredients comprising what I hastily dubbed Texas Stew for lack of a proper name when April asked what it was. How could she care? And how could she greet me so graciously when I brought it over that I left feeling as though I'd been the most important of the many persons in her house that night? Of course, she was that gracious with everyone, a lady all the way, making each person feel special in her eyes. Even in the midst of knowing that a common, minor winter malady like the flu had stilled her precious son's heart at last. Fate could dispense with some of its ironic twists if you ask me.

Ricky had died in March, and I still had found no words of consolation that didn't sound incredibly hollow and, somehow, false. So I wound up saying things mundane, as though April's world were still right side up and all of one piece, things like "Aha! I caught you playing hooky."

Her head was bowed to the book lying open on her lap, but her gaze seemed to encompass eternity

147

rather than a mere few words on paper. Her cheek rested on her hand. The crevices between her knuckles glistened as sunlight bounced off tiny puddles of moisture, remnants of tears shed before my inadvertent invasion of her privacy. If only my mouth hadn't spoken before my brain got into the act; I could have backed away without disturbing her. Fortunately, it was one of those rare times when my mouth had better instincts than my brain. The smile April turned to me was friendly, warm, and genuinely welcoming, the hand she extended a bidding to join her.

"Margarete, how good to see you. I'm not playing hooky, my dear, it's my day off." Her eyes were puffy and a bit red, but dry. "I was just remembering how good your Texas Stew was. Do you know, we sat up all that night, spoons in hand, eating it like gluttons. I can't tell you how glad I am to have you back."

I walked over and took her hand. She clasped mine with both of hers, gave it a squeeze, and smiled. "I'm glad to have me back, too," I said. "It looks as though I'm going to be spending more time in the yard than the house this year, though. I certainly have my work cut out for me to get it all back in shape."

"I can see that," she said with great sympathy. "It's too bad. My Ricky would have been so glad to help you. Have you noticed how many birds we have around this year? Ricky would have loved seeing them. He used to get a kick out of watching the sea gulls when your father put out fat for them in winter. We were wondering if you'd be feeding them, too."

"I have been feeding the small birds," I said, "but the sea gulls I can do without. They're so greedy! Thank goodness those huge ones fly back to the Arctic in spring. They sound like a herd of elephants dancing when they're on the roof!"

April laughed. "I remember. I remember. The gulls used my roof as an outpost to watch for your father. The kids would look up at the ceiling as if they were afraid it would come down on their heads." Obviously enjoying the memory, she laughed again. "I wish Ricky could have seen your cat chasing the squirrel this morning. He used to get such a kick out of her. I laughed until I cried while I watched her in action. She's spry for such an old girl."

How could she have the courage to carry on small talk, the strength to laugh? We each suffer and recover in our own ways, of course. And though time does heal most wounds, some are so deep that we can only hope to learn ways to endure the pain. We can enclose it in a private space apart from the rest of life; cry enough tears to obscure it; overwhelm it with another strong emotion; take it out, look it in the face, reason that there is no why, and decide that it's simply necessary to continue on—all are ways of enduring pain that will evermore be part of life. Recovery sometimes means achieving a delicate balance between the sorrows and sweetnesses of life, both of which are always present. Remembering yesterday, we reach for every tomorrow, because tomorrow is the reason for there being a today.

April laughed for tomorrow while interweaving talk of yesterday and today and what could have been in full recognition of what was. And I'd had difficulty talking to her because I'd felt it inappropriate to discuss everyday matters, the very essence of life, with her! I'd been acting as though she were an empty eggshell, capable of withstanding only the most careful treatment, when what she needed was to go on living one day at a time. The conversation she required had to be about the normal patterns of life continuing.

As she and I chatted, Arnie's voice wafted through the window. Inside the house, he'd decided the day was too beautiful to pout any longer and was searching for every word and tune at his command. "Peek-a-boo, peek-a-boo, peek-a-boo. I love you, yes I do," he said in his most melodious singsong. "Hi. Hi there. He's a little Arnie. He's a little bitty baby boy, yes he is. Bundy's a bad boy, he is. C'mere, Sammie, Mitzi, give Arnie a kissy . . . "

"Don't tell me that's Arnie!" April said.

"That's him all right."

"Unbelievable! I'd forgotten how clearly he speaks. He's so amazing. So amazing! It sounds like he's calling the cats, too."

"He is. And that reminds me . . . You haven't seen a tiny, skinny black cat wandering around by any chance, have you? One of the beasts went over the fence."

"No." She leaned forward in her chair, looked around, stood up. "I'll help you . . . Oh, look, there's a black cat on your back porch. You have two of them, though, don't you?"

I looked through the wire fencing toward my house. Sammie stood on her hind paws and stretched her full length up against the door. I couldn't hear her, but her mouth kept opening, so I knew she was meowing.

"I have two black cats, all right," I said to April, "but that's the one I've been looking for since early this morning. Monster! Looks like she's had her fun and is ready to go inside for dinner and a nap. I'd better get her in before she changes her mind and runs off again."

"Oh, and here I was, all set for a long talk about Arnie. Your stories about him are so fascinating!"

"Why don't you come with me? I could make us some coffee."

"No, thanks, dear. I'm expecting Nancy—my sister Nancy, not my daughter Nancy. Some other time though, okay?"

"Sure, any time, April."

"Say hello to Arnie for me when you get home."

"April says hello, Arnie," I said as I walked through the house.

"Bye-bye, see you later?" he screamed desperately when I didn't pause at the aviary. "Night-night. You go to sleep? Hi there. Come kiss Arnie!"

I let Sammie in, dished out food for the three cats, and opened Arnie's cage door. He paused and looked around suspiciously before flying out. "C'mon," I said, "help me fix lunch." He cavorted around the living room, touched down on the kitch-

151

en table, noticed the travel cage, and trrrrppped as he rushed from the room. Peeking around the corner, I spotted him crouching on the lampshade. When he saw me, he unfurled his wings, flapped them as though beating off a buzzing bee, and screeched at the top of his lungs.

"Reading my mind, are you?" I said. "Yes, you are going outside again, right after lunch."

Most of the ingredients for my salad were in the bowl before he decided to join me. I rescued the tomato from his attacking beak before he could make it into purée and tossed him a shred of lettuce. He swallowed it and reached into the bowl. "No, don't taste now," I said. "You know you hate vinegar and oil." He jumped over the hand I'd put up to ward him off. With a wolf whistle of triumph, he stuck his beak into the bowl, grabbed a strip of onion by one end, tilted his head back, and started to swallow. The onion protruded from his beak like a sword halfway down the throat of a circus performer, disappearing bit by bit until only the end was left in his mouth. Then he paused for breath. He always paused for breath—and always looked as though he should be choking!—when he ate long strips of anything. Unable to bear watching, I turned my head.

I heard his talons tapping on the countertop and looked again. He'd finished swallowing the onion and was running toward the sink, into which he jumped. Landing on the rim of a soaking coffee cup, he swished his beak through the water, back and forth, back and forth, over and over and over

152

again, washing the offensive taste of my salad dressing from his mouth.

"I tried to warn you," I said. He ignored my comment and continued to wash his beak.

"Here, have a piece of rye bread," I said when he joined me at the table. "You'll need the energy. We're going back outside as soon as I finish." He ripped the piece of bread to shreds, but didn't take in a crumb that I could detect. "I know of some sparrows who are going to love every bit you've left," I said as I put my dishes into the sink. "You can watch them eating it, in fact."

I swooped down on him with both hands, snatched him up, and thrust him into the travel cage again. Wiser now than he'd been in the morning, he hissed at me, jumped to the floor, and thrust his beak into the crack at the door, prying, prying, probing, and thrusting, trying his best to make an escape.

"Trust me," I said. "You're going to learn to love the fresh air and sunshine. Ask the cats. See, they're looking forward to another outing." Lined up at the door, they turned their heads with the precision of a chorus line, looking at me with haughty demand for my services as a doorperson.

Arnie trrrrppped and banged the frame of the cage with his beak. "I love you," he said with all the charm he could muster. "C'mere, kiss Arnie. Bye-bye. See you later."

I opened the door. Like bursts from a Roman candle, three cats erupted through it, separated, and shot in different directions. Bundy wobbled no farther than the patio, where he crouched cautiously and looked about suspiciously. Mitzi streaked straight to the mole hole and took up her statue stance. Sammie stampeded to the far corner of the yard, found the fence and clambered over it, then disappeared. Arnie crashed about in the cage, squawking and trrrpping his protests at being thrust into the wide open spaces.

Manx bounced across the lawn, and Bundy was suddenly just inches away from his nub of a tail, sprinting after the squirrel with obvious determination. Glancing over his shoulder, Manx gave a defiant flip of his tail remnant and stretched out into a series of flying leaps that took him to the nearest oak well ahead of Bundy. Up the tree scampered the squirrel. Up the tree clambered the cat. Higher and higher they climbed, then farther and farther out a limb, until it began to bend beneath Bundy's bulk. Manx stopped, turned to Bundy with a triumphant look and chukka-chukka-chukka-cheeeeed over and over again, announcing to the entire neighborhood that he had a cat treed. The treed cat, still oblivious to his circumstances, reached out a paw and slapped at the squirrel, who reached out and snatched at the paw with his teeth. He gave Bundy a quick nip, just enough to let him know that real rodents don't befriend riffraff, then sailed away through the treetops.

At that point, Bundy noticed where he was. The pupils of his eyes grew larger and larger as he stared down at the ground, tried to turn around on the branch, and realized he could not. "Ow?" he said very quietly. A twig snapped from beneath one of his paws, throwing him off balance. With an "Ooomph," he landed on his belly, astraddle the branch. Both sets of paws locked in place, hugging that meager piece of tree as though it were the dearest thing in the world to my errant cat. "Oooowww?" he said. "Meeeooowwww," a bit louder. "Aaaaaaaaaoooooooooowwwwwwwww!" He looked down at me with a wretched, pleading, trusting, terrified expression.

"Bye-bye, see you later," Arnie shrilled as he huddled on the top perch of the little cage beside me.

"Margarete, your cat's over here." April shouted across the fence. In her arms was Mitzi; in Mitzi's mouth was a squirming little mole. Mitzi meowed, and the mole fell to the ground and scampered out of sight.

"I think this is yours, too," a man's voice said behind me. Ray reached across the fence from his yard, a big grin on his face, a squirming bundle of black fur in one hand as he held Samantha toward me. "I have a stepladder you can use to rescue the one in the tree."

"Nothing like a fun family outing." I sighed and set about gathering the clan.

10 "You're a murderer, Arnie."
He cocked his head to the side and looked at me with beady brown eyes glowing softly, sweetly, innocently. No cherub could have looked more hurt—or more forgiving of the false accuser—than he did at that moment.

"You can quit giving me that look, too, young bird. How can you pretend innocence when the victim is dangling from your beak?"

The mangled remains of the latest fatality hung in bits and shreds from both sides of his mouth. This one looked as if it was—had been—a sweet pepper. Nothing green and growing was safe in the house. If it wasn't Arnie, it was the cats eating my garden seedlings before I could get them into the ground.

Arnie gave the tattered plant a final brutal blow against the tabletop, swallowed a bite, and dropped the remains. I watched, waiting to see if there would be indication of some minor remorse in his starling soul. He wiped his beak on a napkin. Looked at me. And glibly snatched another seedling. Chortling, he danced, waving his trophy in triumph.

"Not that one, Arnie!" I grabbed at the plant. He side-stepped. "You have no idea how many animals die from eating common plants—I'm not talking about the ones executed by their owners for the offense, either. Those tomato leaves are poisonous!"

Like a toddling human, he put everything new and different into his mouth: straight pins, staples, slivers of glass, splinters of wood—he found them all in cracks and crevices of the floor and furniture or buried in the pile of the rug. By now, he knew that the most certain way to persuade me to play with him was to find a potentially dangerous toy and threaten to swallow it. When I grabbed again, he ran to the other side of the table.

"I'll get it, Margarete," Travie said from behind me. "I know a trick." He tore a corner from a magazine cover, rattled the paper loudly, then stuck it between his fingers and put his hand palm down on the corner of the table. Arnie jumped into the air, flapped his wings, and dropped back to the tabletop. He ran toward us, gave the tomato seedling another good shake, and struck a derring-do pose.

We didn't move. Travie wiggled the piece of paper. Arnie cocked his head, looking at my grandson's hand with a mingling of interest and suspicion. Again, the paper moved, ever so enticingly. Arnie galloped across the table, thrust his beak between Travie's fingers, and pried them open, dropping the plant. I snatched it.

"Clever thinking," I said.

"I just thought the way Arnie would think," he said with a modest shrug, then grinned. "But you do have to be clever to outthink him! When is David coming?"

"He's not. Teenagers have very busy schedules, especially at the end of the school year." I didn't have the heart to tell him that David wasn't exactly eager to play games with someone so young.

"C'mon, Arnie. C'mon, Bundy. Let's watch cartoons. I guess you're the only friends I have here." The way he walked, you'd think he had a barbell on his shoulder instead of a four-ounce starling.

He needed playmates, of course, but there was no one around to fill the bill. In a few weeks there would be, as local schools adjourned and the summer people began to arrive, but Travie would be leaving for his half summer with his father right when the Cape Cod season was just beginning.

Yet I was determined that he would have a wonderful time. As he grew, I wanted him to feel that this was the location of our family roots, one place he could always call home no matter where he was taken by the mobile ways of modern society. He'd never feel that way, though, if he didn't have fond memories to look back on from his visits, so I'd best get busy dispelling the boredom.

"C'mon, Travie," I said. "You can watch cartoons another time. Right now the fish are biting off the jetties."

His face brightened. "I'll get the gear out of the shed," he said, and he was off and running like a horse leaving the starting gate.

"Wait! Don't go outside with Arnie on your shoulder!!"

Too late. In his excitement, he was out the door and off the porch before I finished speaking. The door swung wide, reached the limits imposed by the automatic closer, and started back to its place within the frame. Arnie looked around, flattened himself against Travie's neck, squawked loudly, then flung himself into the air. His wings beat frantically at the air, his beak flew open to gulp in oxygen, his body assumed the shape of a dart as he hurled forward fast enough to break every starling speed record.

With horror I realized that he and the rapidly closing door were in a dead-heat race for the same space. It was a nightmare scene: the door was going to beat him by scant centimeters and it was going to close in his face and Arnie was going to crash into it at full throttle and he was going to break his neck and die instantly and there was nothing I could do about it because my voice would not work to scream a warning and my feet seemed glued to the floor as I tried to run, tried to catch the door, tried to save Arnie.

Inches short of the jamb, the safety feature of the automatic closer engaged. The door jerked to a stop. There was still a crack of an opening. Toward which Arnie hurtled. With a sigh, the automatic closer released the door. Arnie swerved, turned sideways, and streaked through the narrow space, just as the aluminum edge of the door surged at him. He screeched loudly, his eyes reflecting panic. The door closed. His limp body hung, pinioned between door and jamb.

Travie's eyes bulged as they stared through the door glass. His features crumbled, his mouth fell open, the color drained from his face. His hand, on its way to grab the doorknob, froze in midair. He, too, was paralyzed by shock, unable to move.

Arnie, it seemed, was the only one of us capable of action, With a mighty flapping of his wings, he struggled free and shot across the room, trrrppping angrily as he careened into the aviary.

Protruding from the crack between the tightly closed door and its frame was a clump of feathers.

"Bad, bad, bad, bad, bad, badbadbadbad-badbadbadbadbad," Arnie sputtered. He fluffed, shook his feathers, looked over his shoulder. And stared. Then gently combed the two feathers remaining at either side of the large gap where his handsome tail had been.

"Maybe we could poke them back into place, Margarete, like a hair transplant?" The color was returning to Travie's face as he stared at the feathers in his hand.

"Awwwwwwwwwww. He's a little bitty baby

boy. C'mere, gimme kiss," Arnie said plaintively. Then he hopped down to the bottom of his cage, took a long drink of water, and began to eat.

"I think he'll be okay," I said. "He's due for a molt soon and would have lost them anyway. He'll probably have a whole set of new ones before you leave."

"Can we wait and go fishing tomorrow, Margarete?" Travie asked. "Arnie might need us today. You know, in case he wants to cry on someone's shoulder."

"Fine with me," I agreed with a relieved sigh. All things considered, Arnie seemed little the worse for wear, but I'd just lost ten years off my life and could do with a chance to recuperate before trying to keep up with an eight-year-old clambering over barricades and boulders while salt spray nibbled amiably at our shoes.

In the days that followed we more than made up for that one lost excursion, going to our favorite spot at each tide's turning. With uncanny instinct, Travie hooked everything that so much as bumped his bait, while I bemoaned my propensity for simply feeding the fish. Of course, it's time-honored tradition that the one who doesn't catch the fish must clean and cook them, so I wasn't totally useless. Our taste for the eating wasn't as great as his skill at the catch, though; my freezer soon groaned at the hinges again as we filled it with flounder, tautog, and scup. Boys cannot live on fishing alone, however. And certain grandmothers are remarkably susceptible to the hypnotic lure of: "The space in-

vaders are here, Margarete! Shoot! Shoot! Shoot!!
Watch it, here comes another wave."

Ooo-oo, oooo-oo, ooo-oo, ooo-oo. The space invaders wailed with sound effects intended to disheart-
en the most hardened survivor of *The War of
the Worlds. Ka-showww, ka-showww, ka-showww*
countered my lasers. "Funny, I always thought lasers were silent," I said absently, concentrating on
my aim.

"Uh-uh," Travie replied. "This is modern tech-
nology, you know. I guess it's hard to get used to
after you've grown up with plain old bullets and
bombs, huh?"

"Uh, well, to tell you the truth, I never really got
used to bullets and bombs, either. Arnie, no fair!
Go help Travie. You're spoiling my aim."

"Peek-a-boo," he said, hopping to Travie's con-
trols. *Peck-peck-peck-peck-peck* tapped his busy
beak on the plastic casing as he tried to take over
the game. Travie moved his thumb to give him a
clear shot at the red action button. *Peck. Ka-
showwww. Peck. Ka-showww. Peck. Ka-showwww.
Peck. Ka-showwww.* He mowed down one flying
saucer after another.

"I give up," I said. "Even the bird is better at this
than I am."

Travie giggled. Then said, "No he's not. Really,
Margarete, you're pretty good. Could we quit after
this game? I have to water my tree."

His tree. He was so proud of it. A week after his
arrival, the UPS truck had delivered the fruit and
nut trees I'd ordered. While we planted them, I told

Travie my favorite tree story. In 1973 I'd gone to my native Germany for a visit, a good part of which I spent with my friend Anni in Brannenburg, a Bavarian village. Each day we'd taken long walks through dark spruce forests, trudged up gently ascending mountains, and meandered back to Brannenburg through well-tended farmland. Along the way I noticed many trees laden with little round balls growing at the ends of long stems. I asked Anni what kind they were. She looked, laughed, and said, "Kirschekernbaum." *Cherry pit tree?* I thought with perplexity. Anni explained that the amsel, a European blackbird, always stripped the fruit and left the pits dangling. No one begrudged the amsel its cherries though, regarding them as fair payment for the bird's exceptionally beautiful song.

"Cherrypittree!" Travie laughed. "I wish I could have seen that. If I had a cherry tree, I'd leave the fruit for the birds so I could have a Kirschekernbaum, too."

"This is a cherry tree we're planting now," I said.

"It is?" He gave me his most beguiling smile. "Can I have it? Can this one be my special tree?"

"Well, sure, darling, but I don't think it'll do very well in Florida. Cherry trees like a colder climate, I think."

"Not to take to Florida, to have here. This is my home away from home, you know. I'll take very good care of it, I promise. I just want to know that when it grows up, I can leave the cherries for the birds so they can leave the pits dangling for me."

So now he had his own tree, just as he had his own tomato, watermelon, cucumber, and bean plants. Together he and I were learning about gardening. Despite the watering and weeding and fertilizing, though, that poor garden was one sorry sight, except for Travie's plants, all of which were thriving. I studied his thumbs when he wasn't watching, trying to see if I could detect some trace of green around the nails or the crevices of the knuckles. Maybe the magic lay in the obvious delight he took in the little things, like the first buds showing on each plant, the bees carrying pollen from one flower to another, the swelling of the fruit as each spent blossom fell. He gave daily progress reports to Arnie and Bundy as they assembled Legos together.

"He has to be bored, thought he won't admit it," I worried to M.A. in one of our phone conversations.

"Maybe he's happy to be bored for a change, Maa-gret," she said. "Unless Hanna's changed, she probably keeps him so busy the rest of the year that he's glad to be bored when he's with you."

"Maybe you're right," I said.

"Don't worry so much. How many little boys have a talking bird for a playmate? He's probably the center of attention at school when he tells about his summer vacations. My mother says hello to Arnie."

"Even so, he needs human companions his own age." This time I fretted to Patsy.

"He'll have them soon," she said. "My boys are coming from Maryland next week. "Joshua's just a baby, of course, but Christopher is nine and Michael is seven. They'll get along wonderfully with Travie."

"You're a liar!"

"No I'm not."

"You are so. My brother wouldn't call you names for nothing. Liar!"

"I am not! I don't tell lies."

"So much for the boys getting along wonderfully, Patsy," I said.

The heat of the argument out on the water carried their voices to us even over the lapping of the waves, the screeching of sea gulls, and the boisterous yelling of dozens of other playing children. The beach near Patsy's home in North Falmouth had a shallowly sloping shelf and a sandbar, much better for young children than the one near my place, and that fact was reflected in the crowd there now. Older children and younger adults were scarce among our gathering of grandmothers and grandchildren.

"They're just being boys, Margarete. Don't worry, they'll be laughing together any time now." Kitzi, speaking with the sage wisdom of her experience with three sons, was the youngest adult on the sand at the moment, and she was in her thirties.

In her thirties! Kitzi? Already? Well, so was Hanna. Patsy and I sighed wearily when we thought about their ages. Just went to show how far back we all went. It was a warming thought to know that our grandsons were becoming third-generation friends now—if they didn't become mortal enemies

165

before the day was over.

"He does so!"

"Impossible."

"Nobody likes a liar, you know."

"Margarete! Margarete, please tell them I'm not lying," Travie called as the three boys splashed through the water toward us.

"He's not lying," I said. "Now, why is everyone yelling? And what are you not lying about, Travie?"

"They don't believe me about Arnie, that he's a wild bird and that he can talk. Tell them, Margarete, tell them what a real superbird he is."

"Buuurd," young Joshua echoed, pointing at a wheeling sea gull with his sand shovel. "Come buuurd," he called to it.

"You're coming to my house for a cookout tomorrow, boys," I said. "You'll meet Arnie then and know if Travie's lying or not."

I should have known better than to put Travie's reputation on the line. As Michael and Christopher stared through the screen at Arnie the next day, all he did was stare back at them. Not one word would he utter. Naturally, the boys weren't going to dispute me, but they had a way of looking out of the corners of their eyes at Travie that made him squirm uncomfortably.

"C'mon, Arnie," he kept saying, desperation growing with each repetition of the plea. "He's a little bitty baby boy, Arnie. See you soon, baboon. C'mere, gimme a kiss. Say something, Arnie. Say anything! Coo-coo, peek-a-boo, anything will do."

"Peek-a-boo," Joshua said, putting his hands

over his eyes and staring through his fingers. He toddled to the aviary and turned his face up to Arnie. "Peek-a-boo, buuurd, peek-a-boo."

"Peek-a-boo," Arnie said. "Peek-a-boo, I see you, I love you, yes I do. C'mere, gimme a kiss." He hopped to a lower perch, where he was at eyeball level with Joshua.

"Peek-a-boo, buuurd," Joshua chortled, tugging at Kitzi's dress hem and pointing. "Mama, Mama! Buuurd! Peek-a-boo."

"He's a little bitty baby boy, yes he is," Arnie said and whistled a few bars from Beethoven's Fifth.

Christopher and Michael were convinced and a bit impressed, but they were busy building a new friendship, and Travie hadn't even begun to show them around his territory. While the three of them checked out the video game and Legos and books and puzzles and posters in Travie's play area, Joshua sat on the floor and stared at Arnie. Who stared back at him. I'm not sure who was more enthralled—Joshua, who'd never seen a bird so close up before and certainly never dreamed that birds could talk, or Arnie, who'd never seen a baby before and undoubtedly never dreamed that humans came in such tiny sizes. When he started to peck on his screening, there was no doubt in my mind what that inquisitive bird wanted.

"You want to come outside, Arnie?" I asked.

He looked at me as though I was dumb, waited with cocked head for me to do his bidding, then banged insistently at the screening to let me know I was much too slow for his hastiness.

"Let him out, Margarete," Kitzi said. "Joshua's very gentle with animals."

I opened the aviary door and Arnie hopped to the floor, marched to Joshua's foot, inserted his beak between two chunky baby toes, and pried them apart. The owner of the toes screwed up his face while pondering how he should react. Wobbling on his feet, he sat down hard on his diapered bottom, then leaned forward for a closer look at the action. Arnie tested the strength of two more toes.

Joshua pointed at him, looked to his mother, said, "Buuurd, Buuurd tickles!" and giggled.

The "buuurd" looked to the sound, jumped onto the baby's foot, pranced up his leg, hopped up and clung to his shirt, gently placed his mandibles into Joshua's mouth, parted his lips, and peered into the orifice. Satisfied with the four teeth he saw, he fluttered to Joshua's head and launched into a song. After another peal of giggles and the comment "Buuurd kiss," Joshua settled back and listened with a smile.

"I think it's love at first sight," Patsy said.

As, indeed, it proved to be. "My buuurd?" Joshua asked when they left that afternoon. It took some doing to convince him that Arnie would be happier staying with me than going with him. And in the days that followed, Patsy and I had not a single phone conversation that didn't include Joshua on the extension line, asking about Arnie. "He has a toy telephone, you know," Patsy confided. "And I think most of his conversations are either with or about Arnie. He's a smitten young man."

That day was the high point of Arnie's summer. His molt set in just as temperatures shot to unusual highs for the Cape. The only thing that took his mind off the heat was the irritating itch of new feathers emerging all over his body. In his misery, he became mute; the only sounds of which his vocal cords seemed capable were the trrrpps and hisses and queeks with which he expressed annoyance. Of course, if Arnie had been living like other starlings, he'd have been so busy simply staying alive that he'd have had precious little time to even think about his molting process, but he was pampered and often bored. Like an idle person afflicted with poison ivy rash, he was driven to distraction because he had the leisure to think overmuch about himself.

"Maybe we could train Bundy to chase him," Travie said with a twinkle in his eye. "That would take his mind off his feathers."

I glowered to let him know I didn't find his brand of humor very funny. "Bundy is already doing entirely too much chasing, thank you."

As he was. Some creatures learn by their mis-

169

takes; some are so stubborn they feel that if they keep repeating the same one, they'll get it right eventually. Bundy didn't even care that he was the laughingstock of the local squirrel population. I would have been willing to bet that Manx and his family were inviting other squirrels about town to come to watch how neatly they were able to tree the cat. Each time Bundy culminated a chase by becoming trapped in a precarious position on some lofty branch, the surrounding trees were filled with staring squirrels, all chit-chit-chit-cheeing in time to rapidly waggling tails. They gave the distinct impression they were applauding the performance.

And as if the squirrels weren't humiliating enough, Bundy had discovered rabbits, which have a way of getting into nooks and crannies and crevices that prove to be throughways for them but dead ends for the pursuing enemy. Between the trees and the brush piles and the thorny tangle of wild raspberry canes I was allowing to cover one corner of the yard, Vagabond was repeatedly trapped somewhere that summer, and Travie was constantly crawling or climbing to his rescue.

"You're going to have to learn, Bundy," I scolded at least a thousand times. "Travie will leave soon and I may not help you."

Travie wrinkled his nose, said, "Ssshh," and put his hands over his ears, a typical reaction to the least mention of his departure. It wasn't that he didn't want to go home, because he did; he just didn't want to have to leave to do it. "I wish we could all live in the same place," I overheard him confide to

Arnie later. "You're lucky, you know, that you don't always have to go someplace and change your whole routine so you can be with everyone you love. Being a kid is the pits."

Ah well, partings can be eased with plans for the next get-together, and they give us perfect excuses for parties. Naturally, we had to have one so Travie could bid farewell to his new friends.

While he and Christopher and Michael crammed in every single "last chance to . . . " imaginable, Joshua played with Arnie and we grown-ups chatted; at least Kitzi and I chatted. Patsy was quiet, her face reflecting troubled thoughts. I'd noticed her pensive moods for weeks, but we hadn't discussed it yet. We wouldn't, either, until she was ready to do so. I'd learned early in our friendship that she would bide her time and mull things over thoroughly before she'd make an opening for discussion of her worries. Judging by the length of her silences today, I knew she was mulling extra hard. Wanting to cheer her up, I decided a change of scenery was in order.

"Let's sit on the patio," I said. "It's too nice to stay indoors."

"Arnie, too?" Joshua asked.

"Joshua, you know Arnie won't go outside," Kitzi said. "And it's time for your nap. Lie down on Margarete's bed and I'll tell you a story. Okay?"

"Buuurd so-we?" he asked.

Kitzi's eyes rolled, but she smiled. "A bird story," she said.

Patsy and I settled into chairs on the patio and

171

surveyed the puny results of my novice attempt at gardening. "Wait until next year," I said. "It's a new challenge, and I don't give up easily."

Patsy sighed. "I don't either, usually. But . . . I've been doing something that I am tempted to give up on—sometimes, anyway. It's so discouraging." She paused, but I kept my silence, waiting for her to search out the right words. "I've been visiting a bedridden woman, trying to cheer her up. Terminal cancer. Her vision's going, so she can't read or watch TV. Other visitors are few and far between and becoming more so as time goes by. She's so . . . so angry, so bitter. Understandable, of course. I wish I could think of something to take her mind off herself." She sighed again, looked off into the distance, and lapsed into a long silence.

"Is it anyone I know?" I asked. "Maybe—"

"No, no one you know, though you have things in common. She's from Europe, too. Her name is Ekaterina."

Ekaterina? Surely there couldn't be more than one Ekaterina in a small town like Falmouth. "Why, I know—"

"Margarete, can we have something to drink?" Travie asked as the boys ran out the back door. "We sure are thirsty!"

Patsy and I dropped the subject. This was, after all, the boys' day. By the time we'd crammed in a "last chance to" walk to the beach and skip rocks over the waves and feed the swans at the pond and visit the ice cream parlor, it was time for the good-byes.

"You'll be back next year, won't you?" Christopher asked Travie as they shook hands like the young gentlemen they were growing to be.

"Of course he'll be back," Michael answered for him. "Cape Cod is the only place worth being for summer."

"Michael's right, Margarete," Travie said as we hugged inside the airplane the next day. "Cape Cod is the only place worth being for summer. I'm really glad you moved here."

"Me, too." I smiled with trembling lips as I checked his seat belt.

"Take care of Arnie and Bundy and Sammie and Mitzi and Manx and all the other birds and squirrels and the rabbits and all my new friends, will you, huh. And let me know when Arnie's tail feathers have finished growing in. And when he starts talking again. And how big my tomatoes and watermelons and everything gets to be. And make sure my cherrypittree has plenty of water. And . . . "

He was still running through his list of instructions when the stewardess asked me to leave the plane. We smiled our farewells through the tears we'd promised each other we wouldn't shed. I watched the plane take off and disappear into the sky over Massachusetts Bay, then headed for home.

It's a long drive from Boston's Logan Airport to Cape Cod, and driving is the kind of activity that encourages the mind to wander. By the time I crossed the Bourne Bridge, I had exhausted the memories of summer. That left me face to face with the intruding, troubling thoughts of Ekaterina.

11 I think she was a countess, but maybe not; perhaps that was just the way I preferred to perceive her. I'd been a romantic, very young woman when we met, and that's when I formed the impressions that I would always treasure about Ekaterina. She was entirely too enigmatic, too glamorous, too haughty to be anything less than nobility, I had decided. But then, I'd been raised on my mother's recollections of her girlhood in a Bavaria that was still ruled by a king and permeated with fairy-tale mystique. Deep down, I liked believing there's a human hierarchy, with some of us meant to be admired but never touched—perhaps because I so enjoyed daydreaming about what it must be like to be one of the admired untouchables.

It was her accent that drew me to her that long-ago day in Appell's Pharmacy. Low-pitched, almost husky, her voice filtered through cabinets lined with aspirins and cold remedies and liniments and bandages. Though English, her muffled words sang in my ears with the familiar inflections and cadences of my native German language.

I was at the newsstand, leafing through magazine pages in search of something with a great many pictures. Just beginning my struggles with the language of my newly adopted country, I was following my husband's advice about reading things that would challenge me to turn each page, then force me to struggle with the words in order to learn the ending no matter how exasperated I became. I agreed with him one hundred percent, but I also reasoned that if I chose my material carefully, I could entertain myself by making up stories to match the pictures when I couldn't make sense of the words. The brightly colored comic books were tempting, but the characters in them wouldn't fit into even my wildest fantasies—I mean, really, talking ducks and mice and pigs and magpies—how could I give their adventures any credence at all? I preferred my reading material to be much more serious and sophisticated; thus, I leaned toward titles like *True Crimes* and *Frontier Tales* and *Hidden Treasures*.

In keeping with the army noncom's paycheck that was our entire family income at the time, I always perused very carefully before selecting my purchase. Close to a decision that day as I stood in front of the Band-Aids and looked at photographs of the prospector and his mule, I was enmeshed in the excitement of panning for gold in California. Normal voices would not have interrupted that favorite fantasy of mine, but hers was no normal voice.

"Today I vill have a cup of that terrible stuff you Americans accept as coffee," she said from the other side of the Alka-Seltzer.

The regal tone made me wonder if she also expected it to be served in a china cup and poured from a silver urn. Personally, I'd made it a habit to visit Appell's every day because I thought the coffee there was so good. This, then, must be the "other German lady" I'd heard mentioned as another frequent customer. I had looked forward to meeting her, to the opportunity for a conversation uninhibited by my usual struggle to find the right combination among so many unfamiliar words. Hastily, I returned the magazine to the rack.

Working to control a grin so wide I knew it must make me look like a fool, I forced myself to take slow, normal steps as I walked around the sundries counter and headed toward the soda fountain. Words without voice lay on my tongue, ready and awaiting their moment; German words so deliciously familiar that I savored them as my diabetic mother would a piece of candy. I hadn't had the opportunity to speak any of them to someone who could comprehend their meaning in months. Learning a new language by total immersion as I was doing is akin to going on a diet by retiring to an abandoned desert island. Though I was succeeding, I had reached the point where I desperately *needed* to cheat.

"Guten Tag, gnädige Frau," I said heartily, extending my hand. *"Ich habe . . ."*

The rest of the sentence stuck in my throat as she whirled on me, her finely honed, aristocratic features contorted by fury. Her eyes were like blue lightning, cold looking but charged with menace, as she glared at me. Her platinum-maned head was lowered like that of a bull contemplating the charge. With the controlled grace of a ballerina, she raised her chin until she was peering down her nose, the gesture allowing her to survey me from toes to head with deliberate scrutiny.

For the first time in my life, I felt the heat of a blush on my cheeks. Painfully aware of my appearance, I thought of the protruding knobs of my elbows and knees, so prominent beneath their thin covering of flesh. Though I'd been eating ravenously, constantly, since my arrival in America, I'd been able to add only six pounds to the seventy-eight that had stretched so tautly over my big frame when I left Germany. The years of famine after the war had robbed me of what minor beauty I might have enjoyed at the height of youth. My clothing drooped as though suspended from a clothes hanger, and my face was all cheekbones and big eyes. Never, though, never had I felt so . . . so *ugly* as I did in that instant under her gaze.

"Speak English," she commanded.

"I do," I snapped with all the bravado I could muster. "I t'ink you was someone. Mine friend. Mine mistake." My cheeks flamed hotter. I knew that I was making mistakes, and I realized that the more I said the more evident would be my ignorance of the language, but I could not still my tongue. "You are not my friend," it said.

The woman's face softened. "Come. Sit here." She patted the stuffed red leather seat of the stool beside her, then turned her attention to the steaming cup on the counter. "A cherry Coke for the child," she said without looking up.

This twenty-one-year-old "child" with the baby and husband waiting for her at home stalked right past her motionless back. I'd never tasted a cherry Coke, but I was certain I would hate it. As surely as I hated her at that moment.

The hand that snaked out to grab my wrist had the feel of steel—unyielding, imprisoning, cold as her eyes. "Sit," she said. "It is true. I am not your friend. Even so, perhaps ve have things to say to each other. But you must speak English. Even if it is bad English." Her voice was low, almost intimate, compelling.

I glared at her, my thoughts daring her to issue another command. To me. I'd seen too much in one short lifetime of the damage that can be done by obedience to imperious commands. And while history unfolded in all the repugnance of that era, I'd vowed that I would never obey a command. Who did she think she was, telling me to speak English in *that* manner? "Let go of me," I said with the

178

hardest tone I could muster. I lifted my chin so I could peer down my nose at her as she had done to me. Somehow, it didn't work. Even seated, she was much taller than I. Instead of meeting her eyes, I found myself staring at her lips. They twitched at the corners. I lifted my gaze just as she released my wrist.

Her eyes glinted with laughter now, but the mocking impact they could have made was softened by a . . . by a reaching out. Beneath her icy exterior, she hid emotions that I sensed she would never utter. To say them would be beneath her, but I could feel her need as surely as though she were pouring out her heart to me. She was lonely!

"Suit yourself." With a shrug, she turned back to the coffee. I sat down beside her. Unable to think of anything to say, I sipped the cherry Coke. "It is good, yes?" she said. I nodded. We were silent for a few minutes, then she spoke as though to herself. "It is not a good time to be German. Do not remind people that you are. Speak English. I myself vas born Russian, but my family fled to Germany vhen I vas a baby. Then I fled back to Russia when my husband became more Nazi than man. And I fled to America vhen all of Europe seemed to be going crazy. Politics! It is all a game. People are just the playing pieces. Remember, now is not a good time to be German. Ten years from now, maybe it vill not be good to be American. Who knows? Maybe then you vill flee back to Germany. Until then, be as American as you can learn to be. Chameleons vill alvays survive, tigers maybe not."

Between sips of coffee, she counseled me as though she had been my mentor for years and we had now come to the time of parting and she was summing up everything I should have learned during our association. There was a methodical fixedness to her delivery, as though she was mentally counting the points she must convey, points of survival in a world prone to many abrupt changes in each individual lifetime. Not once did she look at me as she addressed her expressionless monologue to some vague point in the space before her.

I listened, though. How could I not? I was mesmerized by the time she had a second cup of coffee before her. She made sense, of course, even when I disagreed with her viewpoints. It had taken a long time and a great deal of pain to acquire all the bitterness that was evident in the things she said. Though I had first taken her to be no more than a decade older than I, our proximity at the brightly lit drugstore counter allowed me to see the fine lines of age around her mouth, at the corners of her eyes, beneath her proud chin. As she dropped the tidbits of history that had marked her lifetime, I realized that she had to be as old as my mother, and I had been born well past Mama's prime. They were so different, though. To Mama history was a fairy tale; to Ekaterina it was reality in its harshest light. There was no room in her mind for warmth or weakness or fun or fantasy.

"Do not forget," she said when we parted. She stared into my eyes then, as though trying to burn her lessons into my soul. "Speak English."

I mumbled something—in English—then walked home, told my husband I didn't feel good, and went to bed. He was very sympathetic, very concerned for the next few days. It wasn't like me to be so quiet. But I could not talk of mundane matters while sifting through the advice she'd given me that day. I weeded and sorted and relegated it bit by bit to files at the back of my mind. Way at the back of my mind. Maybe I'd need her brand of wisdom someday, but I hoped not. I had no desire to exist if I could not live, no wish to live with realities so harsh they left no room for an occasional fun fantasy, for dreams, for laughter. I had noted no smile lines on her face as we sat. Even my young face showed the early creases of smile lines, and I had, after all, lived through a war from which she had fled. Survived it. With a zest for life intact.

I took up softball. Developed a taste for apple pie almost as strong as the one I'd always had for strudel. Began to read newspapers instead of picture-laden magazines. Learned English as well as anyone once past the peak of ability for acquiring new languages could. And proceeded with building my new life—a very American life.

I saw her often after that, but neither of us spoke of that day or of any subject deeper than the state of the weather. Always in English, of course. Over the years, she collected things—property, jewels, works of art, objects of ready value—just as she had advised me to do. I never saw her speak to anyone at any great length, never heard her laugh, never knew of anyone with whom she became intimate;

181

that would have been contrary to her philosophy for survival.

We never became friends.

I did, however, have one, and only one, glimpse into her private life. Quite without intention, I walked into her home one evening as the guest of someone who'd been invited there to a dinner party. I had accepted the invitation without knowing who my hostess was to be.

It was like a museum, that house of hers. Of course. Fine hand-painted china and etched crystal on display inside heavy, dark oak, glassed cabinets; porcelain dolls and statues; paintings protected from every source of light; tapestries faded only slightly by the centuries—all manner of collectibles hid the walls from view and dominated the tops of occasional tables. The floor was covered by Persian rugs. I couldn't help speculating about what she must have tucked out of sight, tightly locked up for protection somewhere in the house. She wouldn't be one to trust banks, I thought.

As it turned out, she was a wonderful hostess, and the evening became one I would long remember. Not so much for the excellence of the dinner party, though, as for the special piece of her life she chose to share with me.

"Come," she said from behind me as I tried to decide which conversational group to join after the meal. Her hand, at my elbow, was already nudging me along. "There is something I vould show you."

Puzzled, I put down my dessert plate and followed her down a long hallway to the back of the house. With me close on her heels, she turned to the left through the last doorway leading off the hall, and we entered a huge room that I guessed was a closed-in porch. In the middle of the flagstone floor was a seven-tiered marble fountain. Water bubbled gently from its top, spilling over the edges of each individual basin, then disappearing into a drain at the bottom. A single wooden rocking chair with a small, round, marble table beside it were the only accommodations for human comfort. The remainder of the room was devoted to plants and birds. Cages of every size and description were arranged everywhere, their covers drawn for the night.

"This is my refuge," she said. "This is my joy." Her face showed it; for once she looked serene.

I supposed that the cages contained an assortment of canaries or parakeets or parrots, the pet-shop birds people usually choose for diversion. I was wrong. As she lifted each curtain to show me the occupants, she told me their names and something about each—how long this one had been with her, how that one had come to her, the strange favorite food of another. She cooed and spoke softly to each before enclosing it for the night again. Some responded with soft chirps or peeps. Her charges included robins and sparrows and blue jays and quails and house finches, a mockingbird, a crow, a cardinal. All had been either injured or orphaned and were consequently hand raised by a human being—in most cases, Ekaterina.

"So now you see," she said. "It vill be our secret,

yes?" With a gesture of her hand, the change of her face back to its normal rigid expression, she silenced all discussion and led me back to the dinner guests.

Just as we never spoke of our first meeting, we never discussed her little secret. I couldn't understand why she regarded it as such, but she did; her eyes, her manner, consistently reminded me of that fact. I managed—just barely, sometimes—to restrain myself from bringing it up in consequent meetings. As reward for my constraint, she'd begun to have at least the shadow of a smile for me, small evidence that I had not dreamed of the sharing of her confidence.

The knowledge of the existence of that room and its contents, of its place in her heart, faded slowly from my memory, but fade it did. Memories do that over the course of twenty-five years. Just as surely as my life blossomed with ever-expanding horizons during that period of time, Ekaterina's shriveled. Though Falmouth continued to be home, I set out to explore the entirety of America, partly in obedience to my husband's army orders, partly to the driving curiosity within me. Ekaterina left her house less and less, eventually becoming a total recluse. The civilized world did not implode within the time frame she had predicted it probably would, and all her preparation for personal survival was merely a squandering of the myriad minor happinesses that make life worth living at all. On her deathbed, Ekaterina existed within the very void she had created to safeguard her life.

I suppose I never would have thought of her

again if not for Patsy. Despite her thoroughly modern outlook on most matters, when it comes to the meaning of charity, Patsy's as old-fashioned as people come. To her, charity is love, the kind of love that somehow equates to self-respect. You do what you can for other people for the simple reason that you're a person yourself. Patsy gives of herself—her time, her energy and labor, her patience and wit and intelligence and empathy—in places where personal touches are the imperative. She does so simply because we are all members of the family of humankind, and it's only natural to extend a helping hand to a family member in need.

So she visited with a lonely, bitter, dying woman, trying to touch her empty hours with a bit of simple human warmth—not an easy thing to do for someone who'd always held human warmth at bay as though it might destroy her. Certainly, I understood the problem when Patsy said, "I only wish I could think of something, anything, to take her mind off her predicament." There was only one possible reply I could make when she said at a later date, "It's not easy thinking of things to talk about when I'm with her."

"I can imagine," I said.

"You have the gift of gab, Margarete. What would you talk about in my place?"

That's when the memory of that secret room full of birds came back with stunning clarity. I smiled. "Arnie," I said. "What else? I talk to everyone about him, and no one's been bored yet. You tell her about Arnie, Patsy, and I'll bet you have her looking forward to more of the same each time you go to see her."

She laughed. "Of course! I should have thought of that sooner. You'll keep me supplied with stories, I know."

"And you'll keep me supplied with material to build my stories around, won't you, Arnie?" I said to him as we sipped wine together that evening.

He paused in the act of dabbing a few drops under his wing, decided to swallow instead, then settled on my knee and listened while I reminisced about Ekaterina. No longer driven to scratch and clean his body all day, he was once again a polite and charming companion. He still wasn't talking, but his tail feathers had almost finished growing, the rest of his coat looked renewed, and the bright yellow beak he sported for summer was beginning to turn winter black at the base. His annual molt was almost completed and, if he followed last year's pattern, he'd soon be chattering away again, possibly with a few new words and expressions added to his vocabulary.

At least I hoped so. As summer's heat cooled and he remained mute, I began to wonder, and to worry a bit. Though I loved him and found him entertaining whether or not he talked, I wanted to make a tape recording of him talking. For Ekaterina. She so wanted to hear what he sounded like.

"You won't let us down, will you, Arnie?" I pleaded as he helped me bag the tomatoes I had stewed the day before. He ignored my question and continued to peck at each Ziplock bag as I filled and

186

placed it on a cookie sheet for quick freezing. I whisked the laden cookie sheet from under his nose and carried it to the freezer.

"You wanna go outside, Sammie, Mitzi? You wanna go outside, kitty, kitty, kitty, kitty?" After the long silence, his scratchy voice startled me. I grabbed the tape recorder and hurried back to the kitchen, hoping he would continue to talk. Rounding the corner from the living room, I noted that all three cats were lined up and staring at the back door as though it would pop open in response to their combined telepathic command. "You wanna go outside, Sammie, Mitzi?" Arnie repeated, looking pointedly in my direction.

"They can't go outside, it's raining," I said as I reached for the telephone and punched a number. "Hello, Patsy. Tell Ekaterina I'll have a tape for her in a couple of days."

I made the recording and sent it along with Patsy. "You should have heard her laugh!" she reported to me. "I can't believe what an interest she's taken in Arnie. Every little thing about him. She tells me she plays the tape over and over, remembering all the stories I've told her as she listens."

One day I happened across a cassette recording I'd made when Arnie first started to talk and sent it, too, to Ekaterina. "I thought she'd never stop laughing when she heard his squeaky baby voice," Patsy told me later. "Her entire disposition has changed lately. If there's a healing power to laughter . . . "

"Is there any chance?" I asked.

"Not at her age, with her kind of cancer. It's spreading fast now."

It was only a couple of weeks later when Patsy handed the tapes back to me. One of them had been in the cassette player next to her hand when Ekaterina's ordeal ended.

"She sent a message she said you would understand," Patsy said. "She asked me to tell you that Arnie is enough joy to fill an entire room."

12 A terrible, strong, obnoxiously offensive odor assailed me when I stepped outside. I sniffed tentatively and immediately wished I hadn't. It was such a repugnant stench that I considered canceling the work I'd planned to do. I couldn't imagine the source—until I looked toward the back hedges.

Vagabond cowered there, foaming at the mouth. His forehead was creased with deep frown lines, his eyes were tightly shut, his nose twitched. A few feet in front of him was one of Edelweiss's youngsters, its black-and-white-striped back turned to Bundy, its bushy tail standing straight as a flagpole. Squirrels mockingly chit-chit-chit-cheeeed from nearby trees as my chastened cat slowly stepped backward.

"Come, Bundy," I called. Even with his eyes shut, he ran to me as though the hounds of Hades were hot on his heels.

Samantha wiggled her nose and belly-crawled under the patio table when he drew near. The leash that had proved to be my solution to her chronic fence-jumping problem stretched tautly between Sammie and the umbrella stand anchoring it. Temporarily blinded, Bundy hit the leash at full speed, tripped, tumbled head over heels, and rolled toward his mother. She hissed, reached out a paw, and hit him several resounding whacks on top of the head. He crawled to my feet and licked my ankle. Tears streamed down his facial fur as he peered imploringly up at me.

"There are limits to everything, including motherly love, Bundy," I said. "And skunk-stench stretches the limits of love for me, too. Guess I'm all you have right now, though."

I held my breath and picked him up. On the way to the kitchen sink, I grabbed a handful of ripe tomatoes from the harvest basket on the table. "This is messy," I warned Bundy. "but it'll take away most of the smell." Holding him firmly by the scruff of the neck, I let water run from the hose into his eyes, then rubbed the juicy vegetables into the fur of his face and body. He stood passively in the sink and endured the tomato bath. I was soaked to my elbows when the telephone rang.

"Hello," Arnie said. "Hi there. How are you?"

"That's very good, Arnie," I called as I scooted

Bundy outside to rub himself clean. "Now pick up the phone and say it again." I snatched a towel, wiped hastily at my dripping arms, and reached for the telephone. The receiver clicked and buzzed as I put it to my ear.

"They'll call back." I shrugged and went outside. There were chores to do, and it was a beautiful day for the doing. I looked around with smug satisfaction at the yard I'd planted with ornamental and useful trees and bushes after clearing the wild growth. Bright reds and yellows and oranges blazed everywhere. What a beautiful season autumn was! After a year back home, I realized that I'd really missed the rhythm of the four seasons while down South. Of course, there are penalties to be paid for the enjoyment of each season. Fall, for instance, is a major clean-up time—mostly because once those much-admired autumn leaves have drifted past the windowpanes, they settle into a pain in the back. It's bend-rake, bend-bag, bend-lift-bag, bend-lower-bag, then back to bend-rake, bend-bag, all over and over and over again. Human anatomy was not created to cope with autumn leaves.

This year's backache was going to earn some reward, however, for I had finally found a use for those awful autumn leaves. In a fenced-off corner of the garden, I dumped every one on which I could lay my hands. Mixed with household garbage, grass, and garden clippings, the leaves were going to help turn my back-yard beach sand into a soil decent enough to support a proper garden. I had discovered composting, which must certainly have been invented as an act of revenge by someone with autumn's annual aches. What I was doing had raised a few eyebrows, however; the magic of organic gardening is not understood by everyone.

"Er, Aunt Margarete," David had said when he saw the four-foot-deep pile, "didn't we spend weeks last spring hauling your leaves to the town dump?"

"Yes, but I wasn't as smart then as I am now. Leaves are a gardener's treasure."

"I have a fortune you're welcome to carry to the bank then," Dieter said. "Who would have thought it—my sister, the leaf baroness."

"You'll be sorry you made fun of me," I said. "Wait until you see my vegetables next year."

"They won't have far to go to beat last summer's," Linda commented with a laugh.

Martha and Chrissie had been more supportive of my efforts, as had Ray and Claire, the neighbors who were currently my major contributors. I saw them in the yard now, raking and bagging, and went to collect my daily dole. "Here you go, Margarete," Ray said as he swung the filled trash bag over the fence between our yards. "You're the first person I ever met who works to collect leaves instead of struggling to get rid of them." Claire smiled, leaning her cheek against the rake. "I know it seems strange," I admitted. "But these leaves are only the beginning of a great garden." Ray swung another bag over. "Well, I wish you luck," he said with a smile. "Seems like you're making a lot of work for yourself, though."

Ray was right—but it was exactly what I needed.

Hard work eases frustration while leaving the mind free to sort out problems. Boy, did I have a big decision to make, a big, tough one that might determine the course of my future for all the years to come.

"Life doesn't play by the rules we're taught," I groaned, gritting my teeth against the pain in my back. "Why can't it be fair once in a while?" I moaned as I unenthusiastically pulled and shoved with the hoe. My belly was already cramping with a warning that I was asking for a full-scale attack of Crohn's Disease, the strange intestinal malady that had finally ended my ability to hold down a regular job. I hated the retirement that had been forced on me by my body's betrayals. "I'm getting old," I sighed. "Old and tired and depleted of the will it takes to survive." I leaned on the hoe and watched the birds bathing while self-pity took control.

I'd thought myself free to create a new life when I finally came home. Oh, there'd still been a few wounds to lick on the way to crawling out of absorption with my midlife crisis, which had caused me to leave, then caused me to return here in the first and last place. But the only wound still not healing at the time had been my grief over the loss of my parents, and confronting the ghosts and memories within this house had started the mending process on that score.

Now, though, I was faced with another specter, one I'd wrestled and—so I thought—defeated not long ago. The prospect of losing all the fruits of one's labors is unsettling at any stage of life, but—

I had to face it—when old age approaches and poverty appears to be the condition in which it'll be endured despite careful planning and years of labor to ensure it won't be so—darn, I'd started over so often already, but youth has the vigor and resilience and time and health with which to battle life's ups and downs. "I'm too old now!" Tears welled, then streamed down my cheeks.

Ashamed, fearful that I might be seen in the midst of feeling sorry for myself, I dropped the hoe and ran into the house, where I could hide and continue to cry. "We're going to lose everything!" I moaned to Arnie, my only witness. Correction, one of two witnesses, I realized when I noted Mitzi eyeing me sleepily from the fireplace hearth. Well, Mitzi had been listening to my problems for years, and whatever affected me affected her. I let Arnie out of the aviary and continued to wail my plight aloud.

"That young couple I liked so much, the ones we gave such a break on buying the house in Texas, they've skipped out on us! Months behind in their payments on the mortgage, owing the taxes, and leaving the house wide open for vandals to destroy. With an insurance policy that won't cover the damage because the place was left unprotected. If only they'd let me know they were leaving, I could have taken steps. But no, they kept calling and begging my patience while they straightened out their own problems. And I coped with it from my end, trusting them! I don't know what we're going to do! Do you know, someone kicked in doors and walls, the ceiling even, and set a fire in the middle of one of the bedrooms?"

Sobbing, I threw myself onto the couch. Arnie squatted on my head, unmoving. Mitzi jumped up, put a paw on my hand, and meowed gently, then lay down beside me. I stroked her, letting the tears and self-pity flow. "My life savings went into buying and building that place. All for a dream, an unrealized dream. Now, if the bank doesn't take it over, the tax people will. We're ruined, ruined!"

Papa appeared in front of me, shaking his head sadly. "My poor stubborn Gretel," he said. "I told you that dreams are for fun, not for taking seriously. Remember my dreams? One of the silly ones was the motorcycle, but, oh, how I wanted it—a big Harley-Davidson I would have. Two of them I wrecked, one when I hit the bump and ran into the utility pole, the other when the cow ran into me. Then there were the ones confiscated by the army. And then—how many—four, five, six, maybe, all blown up by bombs in Munich. Not one did I have for more than a week. Did I get upset because I lost my dreams? I just went out and got another dream. You see, you must not take dreams seriously. Go get another dream, Gretel."

Beside him, Mama tightened her jaws. "Don't listen to him Gretel. Your father is sometimes too practical. You must hold tight to dreams; dreams keep us going when there seems no other reason to live. When I was a young girl, we were wealthy; then came the depression, and we were poor. But I believed in fairy tales and I kept dreaming, and my Prince Charming came along." She turned to my father and smiled. "Even if he was sometimes too practical. You must never give up on dreams, dear Gretel. Never give up. Never give up. Never . . ."

I awoke with a start. Beside me on the couch, Mitzi lay with eyes open but a slit, her face looking as sad as I had felt when I dozed off. Squatting on her haunch, Arnie stood up and stretched when I moved my hand. "Good morning!" he said. "I love you!" I laughed. "Sad as I *had* felt" was right, because I did feel better. Maybe because of the self-indulgent crying I'd done. Tears do have emotional healing power; some scientists say it's because they contain a chemical that the body manufactures in times of sorrow and despair, a chemical that leaves one feeling better once drained through tears. Crying is very healthy sometimes, and—whatever the explanation—it can be soothing.

Or maybe Mama and Papa had done the soothing. There is something of each in me: Papa's practical, level-headed common sense and Mama's whimsical ability to believe that fairy tales come true—both are part of my legacy, a legacy that I must not betray with a defeatist attitude. I'd had a good cry, indulged my moment of weakness, been reminded of the influence of my mother and father, who would, indeed, always be part of me, but I must move on now. Perhaps because I have traits of both parents in me, I've always realized that dreams can be *made* to come true, if as much doing as believing is involved in the process.

I still had that decision to make, and it was a big one.

I could save the property in Texas—if I wanted to, if I had the courage to take the risk. Because Mama and Papa had taught me, and Ekaterina had reinforced the lesson, that it's great folly to trust either paper money or property rights to endure in a changing world, that one's assets must be spread as much as possible so there will always be something to fall back on in times of crisis.

Actually, I'd witnessed enough in my own lifetime to make that hard lesson sink deep. For I've known simple things like postage stamps and loaves of bread to cost millions of marks—or one tiny piece of soap. I've seen money burned by wheelbarrow loads as a provisional government attempted to control the black market by switching currency unexpectedly and often. And watched as families were ordered from their homes at gunpoint for one reason and another. And been allowed to leave my native country with only sixty-six dollars of the money I'd schemed and scrimped to save for coming to America, because of a rule that had something to do with paying a national debt that dated back to before I was born.

It's important to know and understand the broad view of history—not the kind that consists of dates and battles and leaders' names, but the part that tells the effects of events on ordinary people—a history that consists of individual memories not written into textbooks. Because today's certainty is not tomorrow's. And lessons hard learned become habits if one is prudent.

Since I had learned my history lessons well, I had

a few gold coins and a bit of silver tucked away in a safe-deposit box at the bank. That was my lifeline in case of extreme emergency. There wasn't much, but it should be enough to pay taxes and insurance and the mortgage for a while. Enough to hang on for a bit longer—if I wanted to. I just didn't know if it was worth it to put my final assets at risk. It's often best to let go of material holdings, no matter how much it may hurt, no matter the cost.

I'd often thought it was an ill-omened star that led me to Texas in the first place. Five years I'd spent there, working my heart out to build a home and a business and a future. Yet everything I'd touched had been doomed to failure. For me, nothing good had come out of Texas . . . except Arnie, Bundy, and Sammie, that is. Could I expect my luck to change now?

"There's twenty-four percent unemployment here," I'd been told by the real estate agent handling the property. Not much chance of selling it then, and after the vandalism, not much likelihood of renting, either. I was inclined to let it go, but I wouldn't act hastily. Some strange instinct told me to hang on. Or was it just stubbornness telling me that? I may crumble into self-pity from time to time, but I'm more inclined to be like a bulldog defending a favorite old bone when it comes to giving up on dreams. And everything I owned in Texas was part of a dream.

"We'll see," I sighed as I stroked Mitzi. "Arnie, quit pulling her whiskers. You go home now so I can check on Bundy and Sammie. Then I have to get back to work."

"Let's go to work," he said as I put him back into the aviary. "Let's go to work." And that's just what I did . . . that and more mulling. Between the two, I couldn't be bothered with answering the telephone the two or three times I heard it ring that afternoon, and when I'd finished, I was too exhausted to think another thought that day. Maybe I'll reach a decision after a good night's sleep, I thought.

With a groan, I settled into my easy chair with the evening paper. Arnie flew to the top of it and looked at me. "You wanna go outside?" the little smart aleck said. "Let's go to work!" Let him learn a new expression, and he used it every chance he could to taunt me.

"Ha! Ha! The bird has a real sense of humor," I said. "No way! I'm not moving from this chair until it's time to go to bed. Leave me be, little pest."

He flew to the window and paced on the sill, squawking and tapping on the glass. Why did I feel there were eyes on me, that I was being watched? "He's a bad boy. You go to sleep," Arnie said. Wondering what was holding his interest at the window for so long, I glanced up.

Manx sat on the outside ledge, looking through the glass. Two blue jays stared at me from nearby branches. A titmouse cocked his eye at the emptiness of the window feeder, then flew away. "I forgot to put out bird food today," I realized, and it's not nice to neglect the meal when dinner guests come calling, no matter how preoccupied the cook may

be. I forced myself to get up. With one coffee canful of sunflower seeds for the ground feeders and squirrels, another of the mix for the feeders, I made my daily rounds.

As I reached for the last feeder, the lid popped open and the startled face of a chipmunk appeared. His cheek pouches were bulging so much he couldn't even close his mouth. At the sight of my hand reaching toward him, he scurried out and away. "Monster," I muttered, wrestling with the feeder. The trouble with chipmunks is that they excrete as they stuff, invariably making an unsanitary mess. Now I'd have to wash out the feeder before I'd serve food in it. As I struggled with the clothes hanger from which it was suspended, the telephone rang.

"Oh, drat!" I said vehemently, wrestling with the feeder and taking an automatic two steps toward the sound. I tripped over the blocks around the basement window well. And went sprawling. I scrambled to my feet and ran.

I was out of breath when I hit the door, but the

shrill rings were still sounding. I grabbed the receiver, put it to my ear, and panted, "Hello." Instead of the mocking bzzzzzz I'd fully expected to hear, there was a voice reply.

"Good evenin', ma'am. May I speak with Margarete Corbo, please?"

"This is she."

"Mrs. Corbo, I'm callin' from Houston, Texas. I've been tryin' to reach you all day, ma'am. Sorry to bother you, but I'm hopin' you can help me locate the owners of that piece of land you used to own down here."

"You're speaking to the owner. When I sold the property, I had to finance the deal and, well, the couple who bought it got a divorce and everything fell through. It's back on the market now if you're interested in buying it."

"Actually, we had somethin' else in mind, ma'am. I represent Mapp Petroleum Company. How would you feel about leasin' the mineral rights to us? I know you did it once before with another company and nothin' came of it, but this time it will. Our geology reports say it has wonderful prospects. We want to start drillin' for gas on that tract as soon as possible."

How did I feel about leasing the mineral rights? If only the man knew! I had bought land and invested my life savings and lived in Texas for one big reason: I'm an inveterate impossible dreamer. I've walked the beaches of Florida with a metal detector, hoping to find washed-up sunken treasure, and spent my spare time panning for gold in California and Nevada, and been haunted by the obsession of black gold in Texas. An oil well—that's what I'd dreamed would come of my stay in Texas! A gas well would certainly do. I didn't need geology reports to convince me there were wonderful prospects under that piece of land—I'd always known it.

"You're welcome to drill all you want," I said. "Send me the papers to sign."

It would take a while, he explained. There were permits to obtain, and they had to wait for a drilling rig and crew to be available, and no telling how long the actual drilling would take, and then maybe it would be a dry hole. But if they were lucky, I could look forward to royalties as long as there was something worth pumping out of that hole. I knew all that, but let him explain anyway. It was nice to hear my thoughts come out of someone else's mouth.

"Come on out here and help me celebrate, Arnie," I said after I hung up the telephone. "Looks like we're going to get our Texas oil well after all. Some dreams actually do come true, you know. Just takes a stubborn believer to hang in until the time is right."

"I love you," he said. "C'mere, gimme a kiss. Let's go to work."

The next day I would go to the bank, then to a coin dealer, and back to the bank. With a cash deposit. Okay, so it was a risk. Maybe the well would be a dry hole, but I didn't think so. And what's life without risk—for the sake of a dream.

Now I could get on with my life, search for new

ways to flesh it out with meaning, maybe look around for a few new dreams. Even if I had to hold my breath in anticipation for a while. "My oil well wouldn't dare be a dry hole!" I shouted to the animals. "Would it?" I mumbled.

13 Animals are great companions but lousy conversationalists. My news required sharing with someone other than the wild kingdom. Naturally, I reached for the telephone and punched the most familiar number.

"Patsy, you'll never believe what just happened," I started. And barely paused for breath until I'd raved nonstop for a good quarter hour. "You know what this could mean? Why, this time next year, maybe I can actually hire people to do some of the jobs I've been tackling around here: carpenters and plumbers and painters and someone for yard work and . . . and you name it! Doing it yourself isn't all the fun it's cracked up to be when it's mandatory."

Patsy listened politely, as always. Then she just as politely gave me a dose of her level-headed common sense to get my feet back on the ground where they belonged. "I'm very happy for you, Margarete, but I'm worried that you're going to be terribly disappointed if your expectations soar too high. Remember, you told me yourself that even if someone did find oil under your land, you wouldn't have an interest large enough to allow you more than a few luxuries from month to month."

"What do you think repairmen are if not luxuries! I'm tired of having to work so hard."

"Well, if you're going to become a lady of leisure, I don't suppose you'll be interested in hearing my solution to the problem you've been complaining so much about lately."

"Sure I'm interested. What problem?"

"Boredom. You've been worried that you'll be bored once you've finished your projects around the house and yard. I found a wonderful solution for you in the *Falmouth Enterprise* today, but it doesn't sound as though you'd be interested now."

"Try me." I listened, and as she talked, I became very interested, indeed. Some people may be born to a life of leisure, but I don't suppose I'll ever qualify for the category, no matter how much I try. Patsy's idea was right up my alley. But I didn't think I could cope with it.

I tossed and turned a great deal that night, unable to fall asleep in the first place, then waking sporadically to start the process all over again. Insomnia and I were old friends, but it had been a long time since we'd been intimate. Heavy thoughts and old nightmare demons haunted me until I finally forced myself to get out of bed.

Mitzi jumped from her corner of the bed, yawned, and pranced ahead of me to the kitchen. As I tiptoed through the living room, Arnie said a startled "Good morning!" and hissed when he realized it was still dark. Quietly, I gave Mitzi a spoonful of food, poured a glass of orange juice for myself, and sipped it as I gazed through the kitchen window.

A shadow moved beneath the oak tree, disappeared behind the trunk, then walked out onto the lawn. Looking like a hunchbacked cat, it ambled toward the spot where I'd been feeding the birds. A startled rabbit hopped out of its path. Mitzi jumped up, put her paws on the window sill, and swished her tail with slow, emphatic whips. "See, Mip-Mip," I whispered, "all that food you spoiled brats refuse to eat is a smorgasbord to the raccoon." I stroked her head and we watched together while the raccoon nibbled about on the ground, walked leisurely along the edge of the hedge line, and clambered nimbly over the fence. Mitzi and I moved to the living room window and watched Edelweiss digging for grubs. From the wooded lot across the street, a saw-whet owl whistled its mellow too-too-too-too-too-too-too-too.

With all that life going on even in the still of the night, it was hard to linger on deliberations of death. When I went back to bed, sleep came swiftly, peacefully.

"I gave it a great deal of thought last night," I said to Arnie as we made coffee together the next morning. "Patsy means well, but her suggestion isn't for me. Suicide prevention is best left to the professionals."

Perched on the rim of the dish drainer, Arnie looked me in the face while I talked, then turned his attention to what my hands were doing. As I ran water into the pot and measured the grounds, he scrutinized my every move. Feeling left out, Bundy deserted the post in front of his dish and jumped onto the countertop to join us.

"Down, Vagabond," I ordered sternly, snapping my fingers and pointing to the floor. Arnie trrrppped to reinforce my command. I could always rely on him to back me up when it came to disciplining the cats. Bundy gazed at me with pleading eyes, decided it was one of my grumpy mornings, and jumped heavily to the floor. "Ooooowwwwwww," he begged mournfully. "Stop it," I barked. "You're not starving!" Mitzi stood her ground, frowning at me with a look that said I was being nasty to take my mood out on them. Samantha started to slink out of the kitchen. "Come on back, Sammie," I said. "I'm sorry. I'm acting like an ogre. Patsy's suggestion brought back some old, sad memories, and I had a bad night. I'll get your breakfast."

Opening the cabinet door, I stared at the stacks of cans and started my daily guessing game. Arnie flew inside and pranced around on the shelf, scrutinizing the labels as though he might be able to help me with the decision. "If the cats could talk like you, Arnie, they could tell me themselves and save me this agonizing." He pecked at a can. "Tuna and egg, you think? Okay, I'll give it a try."

Once the cats were taken care of, I drank a cup of coffee while glancing through the morning paper. Arnie jumped on the sports section when I dropped it to the floor, registering his opinion of the contents by pecking holes into select stories. When I took too long over the news pages, he flew up and teetered precariously on the top edge of the wobbly paper, peering down his black beak at what I was reading.

"Can you believe it?" I said. "A young man hanged himself from the cell bars in one of the local jails last night. He was only in there for public drunkenness; he could have gone home this morning. What a waste of a young life!"

Arnie ripped the edge off the paper and ate it. "Arnie! That could be very unhealthy, you know. No telling what chemicals are in that paper. You must be getting hungry. C'mon, let's clean your cage so you can go home and eat."

He sat on my shoulder while I rubbed down his perches with a wire brush and changed the newspaper on the bottom of the cage. When I opened a fresh can of corn, he quickly gobbled a few kernels, then flew inside the aviary and waited for me to dish it up along with the lettuce and boiled egg yolk that he'd settled into for his daily fare. No matter how I tried, I hadn't been able to convince him that any other food was worth eating, but I'd long since given up worrying about whether or not his nutritional needs were being met. I couldn't force-feed him all his life, and he simply would not touch anything else. Though I routinely offered everything imaginable, he just as routinely refused it all, so we were stalemated in the matter of his diet. Thank goodness, he was healthy anyway.

"Now the zoo is taken care of, it's people time at long last," I said. With a second cup of coffee in hand, I glanced at the clock. "Right on schedule," I mumbled and reached for the telephone. Patsy and I have always visited over that second leisurely cup of coffee, exchanging news from the different papers we read, pronouncing our judgment on the sorry state of political affairs the country always seemed to be in, solving the problems of the world with our combined wisdom. Once we'd done that, each day was worth embracing with optimism.

209

"Good morning!" I said into the receiver. "How was your night?"

"Good morning," she replied. "My night was fine. And yours?"

"Mine was restless, and it's your fault."

"Oh?"

"Patsy, there's no way I could join that suicide prevention organization. What did you say the name is—the Samaritans?"

"Oh?"

"No way. I think it's dangerous for amateurs to go around giving advice to suicidal people."

"That's not the way the Samaritans operate, Margarete. I've been reading about them since Monica Dickens started the first branch here some years ago. They're in the business of listening, of giving a friendly ear to people who are in the middle of a crisis that might result in suicide *if* they don't find a way to let off steam. The Samaritans' stated goal, as a matter of fact, is to befriend the suicidal and despairing. They're friends in time of need, that's all, someone to listen to the problems of another human being who desperately needs to talk. I still think you'd be perfect for the job."

"You must be mistaken, Patsy. What good are they if all they do is listen? The Samaritans sounds like a church organization. I'll bet they tell people things like Jesus saves, come to our church next Sunday. You know I think religion is a very personal matter. I could never become a closet evangelist."

She laughed. "The Samaritans don't operate that way, Margarete. They were founded by a clergyman, Chad Varah, who adamantly took the stand that a suicidal crisis is the worst time to preach to anyone. He set out to save their bodies so they'd have time to work on their souls. I'll bet the Samaritans were the original hot line. In England, they date to 1953, when even the word *suicide* was taboo."

"How do you know so much, Miss Smarty?"

"Monica Dickens spoke at my Thursday Club last week. That's why the newspaper article hit my eye yesterday—it's all still fresh in my mind. Think about it, Margarete. As much as you like to talk, surely you must understand how frustrated some people get when they're lonely and despairing and have no one to turn to for something as simple and important as listening to their troubles."

"I'll think about it," I said. And we went on to other matters.

In all honesty, I wouldn't have given it another thought if not for my trusty trick back. Ever so deceptively, it sometimes allows me to function as a normal person, lifting and bending and doing all manner of jobs intended for a pack mule, then betrays my best-laid plans by rebelling at the mere thought of a trivial task.

"I swear, all I did was *think* about lifting that bag of kitty litter," I said to the person who'd warned me so often about not pushing my limits. "It weighs only a few pounds, and all I did was open the car door and reach for it. Then I couldn't move."

"I can refer you to that specialist we discussed," Dr. McCann said. Her eyes twinkled and a smile

211

tugged at the corners of her lips in anticipation of my answer. We had, indeed, discussed the matter at great length; she was the kind of physician whose genuine caring concern was a routine part of the treatment, and that meant she always took the time to talk to her patients. Though no older than my daughter, she inspired the feeling that her judgment was infinitely better than my own. I would take Catherine McCann's advice, her good-natured chidings, whatever medication she felt it necessary to prescribe, but there were a number of reasons that I would not entrust the fate of my back to a specialist.

"He would put me through all kinds of tests that I've already had, maybe string me up in traction like a sacrificial lamb, then refer me to a surgeon. No thanks, the one operation was enough. We've been through this before. How about acupuncture? I've heard it works miracles." I knew she'd take my gentle hint for treatment. I towered over her, the figure of authority, certain I'd have my way. It's easy to tower over someone who's seated, of course, when one cannot sit.

"How about something more traditional? Acupuncture has limits, and your particular back problem is one of them. Here's a prescription for the only thing that's going to help you right now." She jotted something on the white pad in front of her, tore the top page loose, and handed it to me. The words, written in an easily decipherable hand, said: "BED REST!! NO WORKING. NO SITTING. NO STANDING. NO CHEATING!" She smiled while I read it, then said, "Maybe you can train Arnie and the cats to wait on you."

"I can't just lie around in bed!" I protested.

"In the hospital you could." Her voice was gentle but firm—very firm.

I surrendered. "I'll go home and go to bed."

Actually, I didn't have much choice in the matter. When one's body will not bend to assume a sitting position, and when one's body contorts as though trying to become a pretzel from the standing position, one is left with only one possible position—recumbent. Besides, Arnie's favorite phrase lately, "Night-night, you go to sleep," was repeated incessantly from sunup to sundown. I wondered how Dr. McCann had gotten to him—surely his choice of words was part of a conspiracy.

There's only one adjective to describe lying flat on one's back in bed: *b-o-r-i-n-g!* Reading proved to be a test of endurance—how little time it takes for the blood of perpendicular hands and forearms to drain into the elbows and shoulders. Daytime television quickly dulled my senses. I could find no busywork for my hands, which have long been more accustomed to the feel of hammers and saws than knitting needles. My nerves were strung too tight for me to be able to concentrate on puzzles. Rubik, I decided in short order, must be an advocate of the devil—certainly that cube of his had infernal origins. The cats curled up with me, but never let it be said that they kept me company. There's little entertainment value in watching felines sleep. Friends came in and out and visited on the telephone for hours on end, but there were twice as many hours in my dull days as they had in their active ones. When my eyes became obsessed with the one tiny spot I'd missed on the ceiling paint job, I knew I was in trouble.

"I'll bet Arnie's lonely out there," I said to myself.

"Of course he is," myself answered. "Why don't you go get him, bring him in to join the rest of the family."

"What a thoughtful idea. I will." I complimented myself.

Easier said than done, of course. I rolled over onto my side—*Oh, groan;* eased to the floor first on one knee—*Ouch,* then the other—*double-ouch;* cr-cr-crawled to the door; and slowly pulled myself— *expletives deleted*—upright.

Knowing opportunity when they saw it, my feline footwarmers sprang to their feet and raced ahead of me to the kitchen. I spooned food into the dishes that currently rested on the table, while the cats waited patiently in their usual spots on the floor. "How many times do I have to tell you?" I said. "You're allowed on the table now. In fact, you have to eat on the table or you don't get to eat at all." The looks they gave each other clearly said, *Wishy-washy, isn't she? Orders us off one day, on the next.* They waited until my back was turned before jumping onto the table, which is exactly what they always did, anyway.

I turned to see Arnie clinging to the door of his aviary. His forlorn look prompted my conscience to

214

give me the good solid kick I deserved. "You've been lonelier than I have, haven't you, Arnie?" My voice dripped with sympathy as I opened his door.

"Bad boy," he said, pecking on his screening.

"No, you haven't been a bad boy," I soothed. "I wasn't punishing you. It was thoughtless of me to leave you out here alone."

He sprang to my shoulder, grabbed my earlobe, and gave it a twist. "Bad, bad, bad boy," he reiterated. "I love you. C'mere, gimme a kiss."

Properly chastised, I grabbed his dinner dish and hobbled back to the bedroom with him. He spent the next several hours bouncing around on my comforter, pecking and prying and probing at everything in sight. The newspapers and magazines and books with which I'd grown weary were still fresh and inviting to him. Rubik's Cube seduced his curiosity no end—it had such a nice tick-tick tone when he tapped it with his beak. The bulbous nose of the stuffed Smurf sitting on the bedside table presented a convenient handle by which to grab the creature for a proper trouncing. Petal by petal—*Quite tasty, thank you,* his smug look said—he admired the flowers brought by a friend to brighten my day. Finding my big toe offensive, he jabbed at it until I tucked it out of sight beneath the covers. When I plucked out a Kleenex, he discovered a worthy tug-of-war opponent in the dispenser top of the box. There was no end to his ingenuity at creating a playground where I'd seen nothing but the trappings of tedium.

"And when he takes a break, he talks like you

wouldn't believe and serenades me with those silly tunes I taught him." I laughed happily as I recounted the day's events to Patsy that evening. "He even stops and acts like he's listening to every word when I talk to him."

"What a difference a reliable friend makes," she said. "That should make you appreciate what a great difference a friendly, listening ear can mean in times of desperation. There was another article in the paper today, with a mention of that young man who committed suicide in the jail and how he could have been eased out of his despair if he'd had someone with whom he felt free to talk. The Samaritans are still looking for volunteers willing to befriend lonely, despairing people. You might bear that in mind the next time you talk to your little feathered friend. Once you're out of that bed, you can't go back to all that physical work you've used to keep you busy, you know."

"It's a delicate subject, Arnie," I said the next time I talked to my little feathered friend. "There are so many reasons that people decide life isn't worth living. I don't know if I'd be able to change anyone's mind on the matter, and if I tried and failed, it would be devastating. I've been through it once, you see."

He sat on the hands I had crossed over my chest, watching with rapt attention as I talked. Sigh. Some memories should always remain buried, but now that they'd been dredged up, they wouldn't go away again. Time dulls pain, but bad memories are like mosquitoes—they bite, sting, leave behind an itch, then return to do it all over and over again. "How about it, Arnie, you want to help me scratch my itch?" Without taking his eyes off my face, he cocked his head to one side, ruffled his feathers, and squatted into a resting position. "Then listen, my friend, and you will hear a tale that's already cost me many a tear."

Maria was fourteen, three years younger than I, that long ago spring. Though I had friends who were closer to my heart, she and I were cousins, and that gave our relationship the strength of the blood tie. That should have counted for something when I repeated, for the dozenth time, "Someday, it'll be just a dim memory. It's all over with, all past. You're young, just a baby, really. Take every day as it comes, just go on doing all your normal things and before you know it you won't even be thinking about it anymore."

I sighed into the silence between us. She stared at a spot on the floor. I kept searching for words, kept trying, but she never seemed to hear me; she never seemed to hear anyone. I was so glad when I was finally able to leave the farm and go home to Munich. Being in that house had made me feel almost invisible. All those silent people—Maria, my aunt, our grandfather—they wouldn't let anyone near their pain, wouldn't look anyone in the eye, wouldn't speak—not even to each other.

Maybe that was because none of them was able to utter the one word on all their minds. It acted like a dam that held back all other words, that one: *rape*.

217

Rape was a worse word to say aloud than a blasphemy, of course, and the prevailing social rules of the era dictated that it cause shame to the victim rather than the victimizer. Maria and her mother had simultaneously been raped by a group of drunken soldiers celebrating victory. Our grandfather had been held prisoner and powerless to help, was forced to witness the act repeated over and over again. In his eyes, he'd failed in his role as protector of the household, a job that reverted to him when Maria's father had marched off to war, then been killed in action.

Much as I'd wanted to help, I could find no magic words to erase the shame those three wore like impregnable suits of armor, an armor designed to hold happiness at bay. Given the climate of the times, perhaps there was nothing anyone could have done or said, but I couldn't look at it that way.

All I could remember afterward was my selfish happiness at being relieved of the burden and my failure to find the magic words that could have kept Maria from hanging herself the way she did. And if I'd been able to stop Maria from killing herself, then our grandfather would not have found her body, and he would not have hanged himself.

As suicides, both my cousin and my grandfather were denied interment in consecrated ground.

It had taken a lot for me to bury that memory. Now, so many years later, I finally dragged it into plain view instead of trying to push it back out of mind. I told the story to Arnie at least half a dozen times in half a dozen different ways, all the while listening for sounds of falseness, of self-deception in my voice. For no matter how I searched my conscience, I could find no trace of guilt.

Finally, after all these years, I saw what I could not have seen then. My cousin and my grandfather had both died of silence! Those archaic, barbaric social rules under which they'd labored had been the cause for their silence, of course, but the real motivation behind both their suicides had been what they perceived as the necessity to bear unbearable pain in silence. How different things might have been if they could have talked about it all—to me, to each other, even to a total stranger.

"If it had happened here and now, Arnie," I said, "they could have picked up the telephone and called the Samaritans. Right? There are times when it's easier to talk to a stranger than to someone who knows all about you."

"Let's go to work," he said.

I reached for the telephone, punched a number, and waited only one ring for an answer. "Hello. Samaritans? Could you answer a few questions about your organization? If you think I'm qualified, I think I'd like to volunteer to help."

"C'mere, gimme a kiss," Arnie said proudly. "I love you."

14 "Is it true that you have a wild bird living in your home?" the voice on the telephone asked. Its owner had identified herself as a reporter for the *Cape Cod Times,* the daily newspaper published in Hyannis.

"He's not exactly wild," I said, "not after living with me and my cats for almost three years. He is a starling, though, and he was hatched in the wild."

"Er, this may sound strange, but, well, I've heard that he talks. There's nothing to that story, is there?"

"I still find it a bit strange myself, but yes, he does talk. In fact, he has a larger vocabulary than a parrot I once had."

Sitting on the back of my chair, Arnie reacted as though I had given him a cue. "Hi there," he said. "Hello. How are you? He's a little bitty baby boy, he is. Yes, old boy. Sing me a song; sing it! *Da-da-da-dum, da-da-da-dum!*" After whistling the first few bars of Beethoven's Fifth Symphony, he ruffled his feathers, pointed his beak up, and settled in for a long session of whistled tunes and singsong snatches of his vocabulary.

"Is that the bird?" the reporter said.

"That's him." I raised my voice over Arnie's. "He uses words and human whistles the way other birds sing songs."

"You must have worked very hard to train him."

"Not at all," I said. "In fact, he's the most untrainable animal I've ever encountered. He picks up some things I say, even things he hears on the radio or television. But hard as I've tried to teach him phrases I thought were cute, he only mimics things he likes. That includes obnoxious noises, like the sound of me blowing my nose and the squeaky floorboard in the bathroom."

"Would you mind if I came over for an interview, Mrs. Corbo? I think our readers would be very interested in a story about your little bird."

"Did you hear that, Arnie," I said after we'd agreed that she would be over shortly. "You're going to be in a newspaper article! No telling how far your fame will spread. The way people react to my stories about you convinces me that I'm right in thinking you're something special."

Mr. Something Special sounded a Bronx cheer

221

and jumped to the rim of the trash can in search of a toy. He inspected the day's junk mail, spotted a piece that interested him, and leaned down to get it. He snatched at it, missed, and leaned a bit further, and a bit further, and just a tiny stretch more—and lost his balance. Squawking and fluttering as he fell, Arnie plunged headfirst into the trash can.

"Arnie, are you all right?" My answer was a loud, agitated rustling of the papers in the can, then a long trrrrppppppp. He fluttered, clawing for a foothold. A pile of envelopes resting against the inside of the can trembled and slid an inch. He hauled himself on top of one and the entire pile tumbled, pitching him onto his back. Sammie stood upright beneath my chin. Together, we stared down at the paper avalanche beneath which Arnie was buried.

The papers heaved. His head popped into view. The hurt and bewildered look on his face would have evoked more sympathy, I'm certain, if not for the banana peel that crowned him like a deflated dunce cap. He gave his head a vigorous shake. The banana skin whipped around, slapped him in the face, and came to rest with one yellow tentacle draped over his beak. Sammie stretched forward for a sniff, and Arnie avenged his injured pride with a sharp peck at her nose. She reared back and the trash can toppled.

Arnie charged out, banana peel intact, and made a valiant attempt to fly. He couldn't get off the ground. Squawking, trrrrppping, hissing, and screeching, he twisted, turned, hopped, and ran haphazardly. The banana peel clung to him with the tenacity of a monster movie nightmare creation.

"Arnie, stand still. I'll get it." He ran under the coffee table. "Please, Arnie, let me help you," I pleaded. "Look at the way you're panting. Your beak is going to come unhinged if you open it any wider." On hands and knees, I chased him and the banana skin around the floor. Frantically, he plunged about the room, dodging around obstacles, ducking beneath furniture, stopping from time to time to shake vigorously, then running again. "You're going to have a heart attack or a stroke if you don't calm down, Arnie! And we have a newspaper reporter coming to interview you. Do you know how embarrassing it will be if I have to tell her you died doing battle with a killer banana peel?"

Arnie ran toward the cats with me in hot pursuit. Samantha lunged and joined in the chase. Bundy wiggled his rear end and was within a hair of leaping when he caught my eye and decided it would be fun enough to watch the show with Mitzi. "Samantha, stop!" I barked. "Arnie, please stop," I begged.

Arnie put on his brakes; Sammie didn't. He stood stock still, panting and shaking; she sailed over his head, grabbed the tip of the banana peel between her teeth, hit the floor, and rolled onto her back. While she kicked and bit and wrestled the yellow monster, Arnie gave a last long trrrrpppppp and took to the air. Rounding the corner, he flew down the hallway and disappeared from sight.

I scrambled to my feet and hurried after him. "Nothing but worry, worry, worry all the time," I grumbled. "Where are you, Arnie? Arnold! Come here!" He did not. "And the reporter thought you were a trained bird," I said. "A trained bird would come when it's called; a good bird would come when it's called. You're an obnoxious beast, Arnie. Come here." When I didn't see him in any of the rooms, I began to worry that he'd been injured and fallen behind a piece of furniture. Then I heard a quiet snatch of "Mary Had a Little Lamb." Was it coming from the bathroom? I walked into it, searching everywhere. No Arnie.

"Good morning! You wanna go outside? Let's go to work! C'mere, gimme a kiss. He's a little bitty baby boy, Arnie, yes he is." His voice, coming from behind me, was strangely muffled. Stepping back into the hallway, I called his name softly, placatingly.

"Peek-a-boo, peek-a-boo, peek-a-boo, he's a coo-coo, peek-a-boo, peek-a-boo, peek-a-boo," he sang.

"Aha! Now I know where you're hiding. Are you going to come out on your own, or do I have to come in and get you, you little rascal?" I crossed my arms and glared at the linen closet door, which was off its hinges and resting against the frame until I could trim it to fit over the newly laid hallway carpet. The angle at which it leaned left a small opening, a perfect entrance for a creature as small as a bird. "C'mere, gimme a kiss," Arnie teased. Lifting the door, I swung back one side and looked into the dim interior of the closet. From deep within its recesses, he struggled onto the top of a stack of towels, looked at me, and chortled.

"Peek-a-boo, I see you," I said. He turned tail and scurried to a back corner, where he slid out of view behind the towels. "C'mon out here, you rascal," I said as I moved the closet door around the corner into the back bedroom. I pulled out half of the stack of towels behind which he'd disappeared. His neck stretched to its limits, he looked at me with eyes full of mischief, then ducked out of sight again.

"I see you," I said. "The game's over. Please, Arnie, I don't have time to play. That reporter is going to be here soon." Balancing the towels, I reached in, swept him off his feet with a scoop of my hand, and brought him back to the aviary.

While I whizzed the vacuum over the middle of the rug, he sang at top volume, trying to outshout the noisy motor. Only by moving quickly did I manage to establish enough order so we could pass muster as a fairly normal household by the time the reporter arrived.

I was admittedly nervous about being interviewed for a newspaper, but I could have saved myself the anxiety. Talking with young Helen Boursier was much like a visit with a new friend. Her questions were the same ones I'd already answered countless times for family, friends, and neighbors. And Arnie was his simple starling self, not the least bit shy in the presence of the stranger who kept jotting notes as he walked all over her person. Seeming not to notice the brightly flashing lights, he gave me kisses and took a bath in the sink for the benefit of her camera. Obviously delighted

225

when he talked and whistled his human tunes, Helen expressed the feeling that it was going to be a wonderful feature article for the paper.

I was therefore disappointed that as days, then weeks, passed, it did not appear in print.

"I guess our story isn't as interesting to other people as I thought it would be, Arnie," I said.

I didn't dare utter my doubts to Diane, the long-time family friend who'd consented, with great reluctance, to try writing of Arnie's and my adventures. "Even the most ardent bird lovers hate starlings," she'd said. "No one will publish a book about one." She'd sent off a proposal to several publishers anyhow and was halfheartedly working on the manuscript whenever her in-progress novel stalled. So I knocked on wood, looked through the paper ever closer each day, and hoped I was right in thinking that Arnie was unique—all the while terrified that his charm existed only in my doting eyes and that Diane might be wasting her efforts. Writers can be such testy people, after all, and I already had my hands full with testy animals.

The cats were at the head of that list. Sulking because I wouldn't allow them outside during the winter, they were in the throes of cabin fever. Tempers flared when they played, and their games often turned into fights. Maybe they were so cranky because none of us slept very well—something kept running across the roof in the dead of the night, romping and stomping, bumping and thumping, keeping me awake and driving them to distraction. I was patient with the cats until they began to jump

226

into the cold fireplace and scatter the ashes onto my white carpet.

I blamed that antic on the gulls. Enticing the cats, their mournful mews and mocking, shrill hi-yak-hiyak-hiyak-hiyaks echoed down the chimney with the hollow amplification of a train whistle in a tunnel. As they sang, they tap-danced on my roof, entertaining themselves until I emerged with my dole of household leftovers for the other birds. I wouldn't have minded their sharing the food, but the glaucous gulls visiting from the Arctic were almost three feet from stem to stern and had gobbling capacity to match their size. What one of them regarded as a little snack could provide a feast for all the other birds in the neighborhood. So I waged war on the gulls by running into the yard, flapping my arms, and yelling to chase them away.

"My" birds seemed to know I was protecting their interests, because they never fled farther than the nearest tree. Even the shy flicker learned to ignore my strange outbursts, but I had a feeling the neighbors didn't. Surely it must have appeared that I was trying to fly.

Whenever I left the house now, the once-friendly squirrels chit-chit-chit-cheeeedddded and swished their tails, as united in protest as a group of angry labor strikers. And those acorns that kept falling on my head—I don't think acorns fall naturally from the trees in the winter, do they? It was my new Audubon Society–recommended bird feeder that had the squirrels up the trees at me. All metal, it had a squirrelproof top and boasted a feeding platform that tipped downward to dump to the ground any occupant heavier than a bird. Though I still fed them sunflower seeds on the ground, the squirrels were convinced there were better pickings in the feeder.

Injured pride aside, they might have forgiven me if not for the chipmunk, who decided it was worth his while to interrupt hibernation for an early snack in March. Light enough to fool the trick platform and small enough to fit inside the opening to the feeder, he sat munching to his heart's content for most of one day, making Manx's gang feel very left out, indeed. By the time I finished cleaning out the feeder in that cold weather, I was ready to join the squirrels in ousting Mr. Messy from the neighborhood.

Meanwhile, inside the house, Arnie and I were battling over custody of the linen closet. He was in and out, in and out, going from shelf to shelf and inspecting as though he was counting the linens. When I chased him out, he circled and flew right back inside; when I ignored him, he settled in for long stretches at a time. Sighing, I draped sheets over the contents of each shelf as a minor measure of protection against his untidy ways.

By winter's end the animals, inside and out, would have driven me to a long vacation at the state asylum if I hadn't been very busy with other things, including the Samaritans.

Along with other new volunteers, I had undergone an intense training course, passed a careful screening of my motivations, and managed to win a probationary period with the suicide prevention organization. Working under the careful supervision of an experienced volunteer, I was taking telephone calls involving all kinds of despair. Many of the clients wanted to spill their hearts out without interruption, to tell their tales of sorrow to a sympathetic ear, and thus to purge the emotions that were causing them incredible pain.

But most of them needed to have another human being reach out and touch them with something as simple as a friendly conversation, to remind them of the little everyday wonders that make life worth living. Almost everyone counted animals among those wonders. Whether the topic was pets or wildlife, it was the most natural thing in the world for us to exchange animal anecdotes with each other. Of course, my tales of woe about the animals afflicting my life met with more laughter than sympathy, but that was quite all right with me—laughter is the best tonic in the world for a troubled heart.

It wasn't long before the sound of my voice on the crisis line met with immediate questions. "What's Manx up to these days?" "Has the chipmunk been around lately?" "Are the cats still scattering your ashes?" "How's Arnie? Has he learned any new words? When is his story going to be in the paper?" "Why haven't I seen his story in the paper?" "Did I miss Arnie's story in the paper?"

The same question was being asked by family and friends and clerks in stores and acquaintances in supermarket lines and strangers on the street. Because I'd told them all to look for it, you see. My big mouth and I are sometimes very incompatible. The nonpublication of the newspaper story was becoming embarrassing. Finally, I picked up the telephone, called Helen Boursier, and asked about it.

"Er, I'm afraid they're not going to publish the story after all," she said. "Someone decided it would get you into trouble if we made it public that you're keeping a wild bird in captivity. It's against the law, you see."

Against the law? To give a good home to Arnie? I've been telling everyone about him! What if someone reports me? What if they force me to banish him from my house and my heart? That would be cruel! What kind of stupid law is that?

I called the Audubon Society to check it out. "The laws are designed to protect wild birds," said the woman who answered the phone. "We're experienced enough in the matter to be practical about it, though. It's almost impossible to return a hand-raised bird to the wild, and you are right, it would be a cruelty for you to even try under the circumstances. Besides, starlings aren't protected by our laws. Only native birds are. You can relax and enjoy your little bird. Sounds like he has a good home."

I called Helen back and told her. "I know," she said. "I checked with the wildlife officer after talking to you, and I passed on the word at the paper. They're still not going to publish the story. Frankly, I'm very upset. They think we're stretching the truth. They don't believe any wild bird is capable of talking."

"Well!" I huffed. "Let's see if 'they' are willing

to put their skepticism to the test. We'll just have to get someone else over here to listen to Arnie and back you up, Helen."

As I hung up the phone, Diane walked through the door with a postcard in her hand and a stunned look on her face. "I can't believe it, Margarete," she said. "I'm working on my fifth book, but until now no publisher has been interested in any of them. I had decided to give up, too, to quit writing forever. Now, for the first time, a real, live editor is going to read one of my manuscripts! Can you believe it?"

"Sure I can." I smiled. "That was always your dream and you never gave up working for it. It was bound to come true. Which manuscript?"

"Oh, I thought you'd know. Arnie, of course."

"Arnie? Really? See, I told you he was something special."

"Don't get your hopes up, Margarete. Publishers are inundated with manuscripts these days, and they can't afford to publish anything that doesn't have a good chance of selling. It's a business, you know, a very tough business. And this is a cream-of-the-crop publisher. Houghton Mifflin is giving us a chance, though. Wow!"

Skeptics! I was surrounded by them. There was no doubt in my mind that Arnie had fallen into my hands for a reason, perhaps so he could touch other people's lives with wonder. What is more wondrous, after all, than something ordinary proving that there's something extraordinary to be found in everything?

"A starling that talks? I don't like them disbelieving my reporter, but this is a hard story to swallow, Mrs. Corbo. I'm here as a believer, though. All I want is to hear him say one word that I can understand."

Arnie was not cooperating. The Falmouth bureau chief of the *Cape Cod Times* was sitting in my living room, waiting with bated breath to verify Helen's—and my—story about his talking abilities, and Arnie was too busy pulling Mitzi's tail to utter a sound. Nervously, with one ear always on that silent bird, Win Schley and I chit-chatted for more than an hour, but ours were the only voices that filled the room. Finally, with a gesture of resignation, the tall man stood. "I'm sorry," he said, "but I really do have to leave." He jingled the car keys in his hand.

"Bye-bye. See you later," Arnie said.

Win stayed a while longer, listening intently to Arnie's every word, laughing over his rendition of "Michael, Row the Boat Ashore," and shaking his head with amusement over the raspy, silly sound of the starling voice. As he walked out the door, he confided, "I had a bet going with my boss over this one. He said that if your bird actually talked, he'd put the story on the front page. Let's see him back out of it now."

Arnie's story made the front page of the *Cape Cod Times* on April 27, along with a photograph of the two of us making kissy-face to each other. Unfortunately, when I make kissy-face at a bird, I resemble a chimpanzee puckering up. Hard though it was, I resisted the impulse to run to every news-

232

stand on the Cape—to cut that terribly unflattering photograph from the front page of every paper in sight, you see. Fame does have a price.

By then, the local story was anticlimactic, though. Houghton Mifflin had already decided to publish an entire book about Arnie. His story was going to be read by people all over the country!

And my daughter had remarried; and the newlyweds were going to bring Travie for a long summer visit; and the house was shaped up into a real home again; and the memories of my parents were comforting rather than painful; and the oil company was going to drill for gas on my property in Texas; and the real estate agent said he had a buyer for the house down there; and my life was taking a new shape composed of family, old friends, and new, as well as a variety of projects and volunteer work I really enjoyed; and my animals, inside and out, were so gratifying—if exasperating—that I would have been entertained if nothing else ever came into my days; and my health was good, my finances adequate to my needs; and it appeared that I was going to live happily ever after!

Which always marks the end of fairy tales, doesn't it? Ah, but real life is not a fairy tale. And my new phase of life, in my—ahem—mature years, had only just begun.

15 The red tulip trembled, waggled, then toppled over and disappeared. "What on earth . . . ?" Before I could finish wondering, a yellow tulip trembled, waggled, then toppled over and disappeared.

Mysteriously, one after another, my tulips had been vanishing for a couple of weeks, but this was the first time I'd actually seen it happen. They'd been clean cut near the bottom of each stem and, since the flower bed was near the street, I'd suspected some young romantic on his way to or from school had been nipping them for a gift to his sweetheart or teacher or mother. Young human romantics don't come in sizes small enough to remain out

234

of sight while committing the caper I'd just witnessed, however. Just beginning to leaf out, the young hedge roses lining the driveway provided just enough cover to hide the stems of the tulips, so my culprit had to be something quite small.

"Critters," I grumbled as I snuck out the door. "It has to be someone from my soup line. Ungrateful beasties!" Tiptoeing down the walk, I craned my neck in an attempt to get a glimpse of the miscreant before he made his getaway. Certain he'd be gone already, leaving my mystery to plague me with its unsolvability, I peeped around the high hood of the Blazer.

Four bulging brown eyes stared right at me. Totally unperturbed by my presence, Manx and a female squirrel stood upright, holding their ground and waiting like statues for me to go away. When I didn't move, the female lowered her upper body a bit and looked to Manx uncertainly. He wiggled his nose at her, flipped his tail at me, ripped a petal from the yellow tulip clutched between his front paws, and chewed it in the most leisurely manner. Reassured, she hunkered back and delicately munched on the tip of the red tulip.

"This is too much, Manx," I yelled, throwing my hands into the air. "This is entirely too much! How dare you steal my flowers? I've had it. Shoo! Go on, get away from here." Clapping my hands above my head, waving my arms in the air, I stamped across the ground with malice in my heart and meanness on my face.

Both squirrels tucked tulip stems between their

teeth and fled to April's yard, then up her nearest oak tree. The flowers were snuggled against their cheeks in the classic Gypsy Rose Lee pose. As I galloped like a lumbering giant after the little, innocent-looking squirrels, my hair blowing in the wind, my hands waving in the air, wrath written across my features, looking for all the world like a lunatic on the loose, a car door slammed behind me.

"Oh no, not now," I muttered. Freezing in my tracks, I wondered how much of my tantrum the visitors had seen. After all my careful planning to make everything go just right today, here I was, supposedly a gentle, warm-hearted animal lover, chasing poor little squirrels up a tree. The slamming car door, I knew, signaled the arrival of Harry Foster, Houghton Mifflin's natural history editor. So far, he'd been only a voice on the telephone, which is what I was presently wishing I had remained to him.

There goes your image, Margarete, I thought. Rearranging my face into a welcoming smile as I turned, I wondered what to say to excuse the strange first impression I had made. Well, there was always truth. "The monsters are eating my tulips. Can you imagine? Invading the flower bed after all I've done for them. Ingrates!"

There was puzzlement in his eyes, a crease on his brow, an uncertain smile on his pleasant face. Well mannered, he nodded his head at my words, shook my hand, and introduced me to his companion and wife-to-be, Susan Meddaugh, whose smile was as uncertain as his. They didn't seem to have the slightest idea what I was raving about. I babbled all the way to the front door, fervently wishing for Arnie to be at his very best. They had, after all, come to meet him, and perhaps he could charm them so much that I would become but a dim memory.

Charming Arnie's first act when I let him out of the aviary was to ignore our guests and fly into the kitchen as though they weren't even there. "Arnie, come back here," I called wishfully.

He streaked past my face, heading for the linen closet; dangling from his beak were the limp remains of a seedling he'd stolen from one of the peat cubes hidden on top of the refrigerator. He chortled as he went by. Before I could make an apology for his boorish behavior, he returned to our company, flipped aside the doily that hid the hole in the worn upholstery of my armchair, methodically ripped out a beakful of cotton stuffing, and flew to the closet with that prize. Chortling.

Harry laughed. "I don't often get to watch a bird flying free inside a house," he said. "Arnie, won't you come here? I'd love to see you better." He spoke to Arnie as naturally as though he went through life talking to animals quite routinely, and he had a wonderful laugh. If the soul of a human is revealed in the eyes, the heart is revealed in the manner of laughing. Harry's was a warm heart, I realized, and we were going to get along just fine. My nerves began to unknot. Began to. Then Arnie flew to the arm of the man who had decided his story was worth telling to the world—and did an unmentionable on his tweed jacket.

"It's only corn," I apologized feebly as I scooped it up and dabbed at the jacket with a Kleenex. "He's not as messy as most birds." Scrutinizing the cloth carefully, I was relieved to see it was unmarked by Arnie's indiscretion.

"It's okay," Harry said absently. He was looking intently at Arnie all the while, seemingly unmindful of all else. "I never realized how colorful a starling is. What intricate markings he has. You're actually quite handsome, Arnie."

Arnie acknowledged the compliment by flying to my ashtray, grabbing a cigarette butt, and disappearing in the direction of the closet again. "He seems to have strange tastes in nesting material," Susan said.

"Starlings are notoriously sloppy nest makers," Harry said. "No offense intended, Margarete."

Nesting material? Nest makers? Of course! How could I have been so oblivious to the obvious? All that time Arnie had been spending in the linen closet, all the "toys" he'd been bringing into it with him—he'd been following his natural springtime in-

238

stincts. Building his first nest, was he? So, my little boy-bird was a fully mature man-bird at last!

I was still pondering that revelation for some time after my guests departed. After all, each spring since Arnie had become part of my life I'd wondered if he was going to get yearnings to return to the wild when mating season arrived. Yet he'd never once shown any indication whatsoever that he even knew what mating season was all about. This year, when I hadn't even thought of the matter, he was finally acting as a bird preparing for parenthood does.

"And just what do you think you're going to do about it, young bird?" I asked him. "There are no girl starlings in here."

He stared brightly at me from deep inside the closet. Eye level with me, he sat snugly in the corner he'd trampled down and staked out as his own. "I love you," he said. "C'mere, gimme a kiss." Then he flung himself out, sat on my hand, looked me in the face with soulful eyes, and whistled "Mary Had a Little Lamb" as earnestly as a troubadour singing a love song beneath a lady's balcony. When he'd finished, he hopped back to the closet shelf, scrambled to his corner, and repeated the serenade in an abnormally shrill voice. Suddenly, all his behavior of the past few months made sense: in his own inept, untutored way, he'd built a love nest in the linen closet and he'd been paying court in the best way he knew how—all for me!

"What do you want me to do?" I asked. "Jump onto the shelf with you and lay eggs? Sorry, Arnie,

239

my love for you is purely platonic."

"He's a little bitty baby boy," he said. "He's a pretty boy, yes he is. C'mere. Kiiiiissssss Arnie. Kissy, kissy, kissy. I love you, I love you, I *love* you, yes I do."

As he launched into "Mary Had a Little Lamb" again, I sighed with sympathy for his predicament and tried to explain. "This is only a young bird's crush, Arnie. You'll outgrow it in time, I promise. I wish I could persuade an older, wiser starling to tell you all about the birds and the bees, but I'm afraid this is another part of your development you're going to have to suffer through on your own."

And he did go through it on his own. I really don't think he suffered, though, he was so obviously enjoying it all. The gathering of nesting material and his little enticements to lure me into the closet with him were all just part of another game as far as he was concerned. Periodically, I cleaned out his "nesting" material, an act that didn't seem to bother him in the least. He just carried in more bits of Kleenex and rug fuzz and cigarette butts and plant seedlings. I didn't have the heart to replace the closet door until he'd outgrown the phase.

He remained as uninterested as ever in the outdoor world and everything remotely connected with it. Maybe he didn't even realize he was a bird. I would never know. Though his vocabulary continued to grow, Arnie hadn't learned enough for us to exchange thoughts and ideas. Or maybe it was I who wasn't learning enough. After all, I didn't

240

know how to say a single word of starling talk, while he'd mastered more of my language than most three-year-old humans. I regretted that fact. There were times when I would sit and wonder as I watched him what thoughts were going through his mind, just as I wondered what went through the minds of the cats, of Manx and his gang, of Edelweiss, and of the other creatures who so enriched my world.

Perhaps, considering the facts of life, it's best that we never learn those things. Who, after all, would want to linger over the thoughts of a cow on its way to slaughter, of a baby seal being bludgeoned so a human could wear its hide, of a rat being subjected to outright torture for experimental purposes? Not I, not I, a part of me said, for humankind cannot live on bread alone and nature has devised a cycle of life that leaves little room for the sentimentality that sometimes plagues people like me. Surely the hawk is never troubled with such considerations when it makes, as it must, a meal of another creature; but then, the hawk kills only out of absolute necessity. If animals have a philosophy, it is far different from our own and infinitely more practical, perhaps even more humane, in many ways.

I'm not alone in my musings on the matter, of course, and curiosity drove me to delve a bit beyond the musings. Because Arnie so often made me feel that he knew the meanings of some of his words, I was making it a point to read articles and books on the subject of animal communication. While many of us who cohabit nonchalantly with animals unquestioningly *know* that they "speak" to us in many ways, it is only in recent decades that the scientists have begun to apply their techniques to finding out whether or not we're right in our presumptions.

A number of dedicated researchers are working with primates and porpoises, whales, dolphins, and other animals on the theory that it may indeed be possible to establish true communication between humans and other species. Though theirs is a young quest for modern science, the findings these researchers have made public are already setting up as much controversy among their colleagues as did Darwin's theory of evolution. Early evidence seems to indicate that at least some animals have complex thought processes far beyond the rudimentary instincts we've long credited as the only motive and guidance for the things they do; and maybe, someday, some form of true communication will exist between them and us. If it is so, then the fine line between the fact and the fantasy of our beliefs about animals is beginning to blur. Could it be we are not alone, even on this one small planet, in the ability to reason?

Food for thought, but anthropomorphic blasphemy. As ideas go, it is far more palatable to say that man is descended from the apes—which is still not acceptable to a great many people, of course—than to wonder aloud if it's possible some animals may, by virtue of intellect, morality, sensitivity, and other "human" traits, have as much right to the earth's inheritance as we. Yet according to our own legends, myths, and literature, humans of every cultural background have *always* yearned to talk to the animals—and have them talk back to us. So why do we approach the science that reflects that yearning with more prejudice and fear than what once surrounded the birth of modern medicine?

In my minor readings, I ran across a passage in a book that I thought explained the emotions surrounding the subject quite well. As Ted Crail put it in *Apetalk and Whalespeak*, "Decriers and defenders . . . are not having a minor quibble about animal talk; they are dealing with an idea so large that . . . it affects our whole idea of the universe and what it is like or should be like."

For who could dine upon a philosophical cow or make a study of pain inflicted upon a rational rat?

As for talking birds, well, researchers who deal with them are concerned primarily with the question of *how* they manage to imitate human speech at all. With such tiny brains and limited vocal apparatus, birds that vocalize with words literally fly in the face of the impossible. Yet there is no question that some of them do so. Bayard Webster wrote a comprehensive article on the subject for the *New York Times* that spring, in which he specifically mentioned two starlings along with parrots and mynahs as being among the birdly marvels causing scientists to scratch their heads. One of the starlings, on exhibit in the Museum of Natural History, said, "Hi, Sam! Hi, kid!" as he flitted about his cage; the other starling was Arnie.

"You're coming up in the world, Arnie," I said after reading the story. "Of course, the article asserts that none of you has any idea what you're saying when you speak, but still, a mention in the *New York Times*—now, that's prestige!"

My prestigious bird grabbed the newspaper by its corner, yanked heartily, and tore the story in half. Stretching his neck to look around the corner into the kitchen, he said, "You wanna go outside, kitties?" The three cats were lined up at the back door, staring at the knob with bored patience. Obviously, they were failing to communicate their wants to me, and the timing of Arnie's words was coincidental. Unfettered by scientific strictures, I delighted in the entertainment value of my own romantic conclusions. I respect the scientists and their ways, of course, but amateurs have more fun.

"This amateur has to put aside her little studies until the quiet winter months, though," I said as I let the cats out and noted the sun shining for the first time in almost a week. Starlings, redwing blackbirds, and grackles were busily probing in the unplanted earth of the garden as well as the yard, gathering food for their nestlings and taking care of potential insect problems for me. A Baltimore oriole was singing from a nearby tree, his melodious song almost harmonizing with the gentle tinkling of April's wind chimes.

I saw Ray working in his yard and waved. Claire's daffodils and tulips blazed with bright color, mocking the empty stems in my own flower bed. For the life of me, I couldn't understand why the squirrels thought my tulips were tastier than anyone else's, but they did. There must have been thousands of tulips within the one-block area surrounding my house, and not a petal had been touched anywhere except in my yard. Oh well, if they took from me, perhaps it was because they mistook the flowers as an offering, like the sunflower seeds I put out for them. I couldn't stay angry with the squirrels; they repaid me amply with their entertaining performances throughout the year.

I noted with satisfaction that the peas and lettuce and spinach, the cauliflower and cabbage and broccoli were looking quite perky. It really was going to be a super garden this summer, one that would redeem my shame of the year before—if I quit wasting so much time with my reading and finished what must be done.

First things first: I got out the wheelbarrow and a few tools, determined to spread compost over the unused portion of the garden so it could be tilled into the earth. Trundling with my load of paraphernalia past the mole hole, I noted that Mitzi and Bundy were crouched shoulder to shoulder, ears flat against their heads, haunches bunched like coiled springs, tails colliding in midair as they whipped back and forth. I paused to watch. Suddenly Mitzi lunged, beat at the leaves with her front paws, then was off and running a frantic zigzag course toward the back of the yard. Bundy, shorter of leg and bigger of bulk, was slower than she, but right on her tail. I couldn't see what they were chasing, but I could hear the frightened squee-squee-squee-squee of the mole that had wandered too near the entrance to its burrow during the day. Abruptly, the parade changed directions.

"No, don't go that way!" I yelled uselessly as first Mitzi, then Bundy, plunged through the netting that supported my snap peas. They tore separate holes through the bottom of the net and ripped several of the delicate vines from the earth, then doubled back to duplicate the damage.

Wrapped around Bundy's neck and trailing down his torso as he ran was a single pea vine, its roots flopping against his left eye, its end tangling about his legs. Just as he was a nose away from overtaking Mitzi, the vine completed its ensnarement. Bundy tripped, fell to his belly with a grunt, and sprawled on the ground. Mitzi smirked at him over her shoulder without losing one pawfall in the stride of her chase.

"Poor Bundy," I soothed as I untangled the vine and freed him. "You're not very good at the cat business, are you? Sometimes, I think you're really a dog born into the wrong body—a big, klutzy hound dog, maybe. Why don't you learn your lesson and give up chasing the little critters around here. You'll never win."

Injured pride shone in his eyes, and there were frown lines on his forehead. He struggled to his feet, gave me a look that clearly said, *I'll show you,* and resumed the chase. Mitzi was still at it, but panting from the exertion of the first good run she'd had since October. As usual, I found myself silently cheering for the mole. Moles, too, helped control the insects that would otherwise devastate my garden and shrubbery, and they were too small and cute to be bullied by my recalcitrant felines.

It looked as if the mole was going to outwit the cats again as they all headed straight for the compost area, which now contained two piles. One was finished and could be used immediately, and the other, a mixture of kitchen wastes, grass clippings, weeds, and tons of newly raked leaves, all enclosed within fencing, had just begun to "cook." Mitzi came to a screeching halt at the fence, and I knew by the miffed look on her face that the mole had found safety by burrowing into the new pile. With a nose-high sniff at the air, the old lady turned and pranced off as though she'd quit the game out of boredom.

Not Bundy. He wouldn't quit until he'd redeemed himself from the embarrassment of the fall he'd taken. With hunched shoulders and lowered head, he stared at the hole through which the mole had disappeared. Then his look traveled up the fence that was barring his way. With cool calculation, he determined what he must do to get to his quarry, gauged the distance, and vaulted upward with a mighty thrust of his muscular hind legs. It was a thing of beauty, that leap, absolute poetry in motion. Up, up, and over the fence he sailed with all the grace of a horse clearing hurdles; spread his legs at the height of the jump to control the fall; landed neatly in the middle of the pile; and disappeared from sight as the loose leaves sucked him under.

I heard a squirrel chit-chit-chit-cheee, then another joined in, and another, until a chorus of mockery was coming from the surrounding trees. I looked up and spotted Manx in April's apple tree and another of his gang on a nearby branch. They watched the heaving compost pile with fixed attention, as I was certain every other squirrel in the vicinity was doing. They seemed genuinely to enjoy every humiliation that Bundy visited on himself.

Ooooooooooooowwwwwwwwwwwwww came his cry of distress. *Oooowwwoooowwwoooooooowwwwww-oooooooowwwwwww!* Every now and then, I could see the top of his head, his frightened eyes, his flailing paws as he struggled like a drowning victim against the shifting, clinging, tightening embrace of four-foot-deep leaves. He began to froth at the mouth, a reaction of pure panic.

"I'm here, Bundy," I said as I ripped open the gate to the enclosure. "Calm down, I'll get you." I soothed him as I climbed unsteadily onto the top of the pile and waded with sinking footsteps toward its middle. I couldn't see him at all now. Plunging both arms in up to the shoulders, I frantically parted the leaves with my hands, feeling for him among the eggshells and fruit peelings and wilted lettuce and coffee grounds buried within the pile. Finally, my fingers encountered something slime-slick but furry to the touch. I grabbed a handful and hauled up. It was heavy. I lost my balance and fell, but retained my hold on the fuzzy-slimy object, pulling it to me as I struggled to crawl out of the devouring clutches of that compost pile. Somehow, we made it.

Kneeling on good, solid earth outside the fence, I cuddled Bundy and wiped froth from his mouth and head. Coffee grounds, crushed eggshells, foul onion refuse, and rotted orange clung to his coat. Mitzi walked over, gave him a lick of sympathy, then recoiled as her nose caught a whiff of the odor. Though compost piles don't stink outwardly, they do go through a stage just before the interior starts to cook when the garbage in them smells like, well, garbage. Even Bundy's lips were curled back, his nose twitching at the offensiveness of his smell.

"I hate to break the news to you on the heels of this misfortune, Bundy," I said, "but you need a bath." As I carried him to the house, the squirrels chit-chit-chit-cheeeed in an obvious call for an encore.

16 "Lady Margarete, Lady Margarete, come hither quickly. Princess Samantha is in grave danger!"

The manner of Travie's speech this summer reflected the fact that he had abandoned the space-age world and opted to live in medieval times, at least while playing at his new passion. He was cool on video games and had put away his Legos, referring to them as relics from his "baby" years. The trappings of his amusements now were suits of armor, swords and sorcery, and damsels in distress. Arnie had been dubbed his enchanted raven, a wizard in disguise who cast spells to help the knightly Sir Travis win his way through one quest after another.

The cats were renamed Queen Mitzi, Princess Samantha, and Lord Vagabond. The name of the game was Dungeons and Dragons, and, for some odd reason, it required an entire suitcase full of books, maps, and figurines to play—and that suitcase was twice the size of the one that held his clothes.

He'd been in Falmouth for only one day, and I'd already learned to ignore his hourly outbursts warning of danger and distress. *Patience. This, too, will pass*, I thought. "What danger has Princess Samantha gotten herself into this time?" I asked.

"Call Lord Vagabond for assistance, Sir Travis," Hanna said. "It's his duty to rescue his mother when Princess Samantha is in danger." My daughter had been exposed to the game long enough to know the proper replies without having to think about them.

"This is for real," Travie said, "and you'd better hurry if you don't want Sammie smelling like a skunk. There are two of them out here. Hurry!"

We did. On the patio, Sammie strained against her leash. Less than five feet from her nose, crouching behind the two tanks in which propane for the cook stove was stored, were Edelweiss and another skunk, smaller than he and with more black to its coat. So far, neither had struck the skunk's tail-high defensive pose, and Sammie looked curious rather than hostile, but there was no point in taking chances. I gestured for Hanna and Travie to get back into the house. They were strangers to Edelweiss.

"You're out early today, little one," I said conversationally. Moving cautiously, talking soothingly as I went, I picked up Sammie, unhooked her leash, and stepped slowly backward. "Is this your new wife? I'll bet you brought her around to introduce her, didn't you? And soon I'll see the two of you parading around with a group of youngsters in tow, right?" Both skunks watched attentively without moving. I opened the door and scooted Sammie inside. "Hand me that can of cat food, Travie," I said, "and a spoon." I refilled two of the dishes from which the cats dined on the patio, then stepped into the house. Sammie, Hanna, Travie, and I watched through the kitchen window as the two skunks daintily ate the cat food, took long drinks from the water bowl, then ambled into the garden and up one of the paths until they'd disappeared behind the snap peas.

Then I stepped onto the porch. "Mitzi! Bundy! Come get din-din," I called. Bundy came out of the shed, yawned, stretched, and ambled toward me. Mitzi pranced up from the garden, and I quit holding my breath. I herded the two of them into the house, dished out food so I couldn't be accused of lying just to get them inside, and joined Hanna in the living room.

"Where's Travie?" I asked.

"He and Arnie have retired to your bedroom. They're trying to figure out a way to fit the skunks into the next quest."

The front door opened, and a tall, dark, bare-chested, hairy man wearing raggedy cut-off jeans and jogging shoes stumbled through. Perspiration flowed copiously from his body, dripping onto the floor; droplets shone like pieces of glass sprinkled through his long, thick, curly hair and full beard. My new son-in-law bent over and braced his hands on his knees, struggling with loud, wheezing gasps to catch his breath. "Hills!" he yelled. "Nobody told me there were hills! Jogging five miles here is like doing fifty at home. I think I'm going to have a heart attack."

Hanna giggled. "The hills are why they call it the Heights, silly," she said. "I thought you'd figure that out for yourself. Don't you remember watching the Falmouth Road Race on TV last summer, and that humongous hill at the finish line, hmmmmm?"

"Don't laugh. I haven't gotten around to making you beneficiary of my life insurance policy yet." Ronnie collapsed onto the couch and drank Hanna's glass of iced Pepsi in one gulp. Sammie climbed onto his lap and rubbed her chin in his chest hair. Arnie flew into the room, landed on Ronnie's shoulder, grabbed a lock of curly beard with his beak, and pulled. "Ouch!" Ronnie said. "Aaar-niee, please, it's attached to my face."

"C'mere, gimme a kiss," Arnie said and stuck his beak between Ronnie's lips. They'd become friends two years earlier and, though he hadn't seen Ronnie since then, Arnie hadn't forgotten.

Looking at my son-in-law's disheveled appearance, I had to grin. Last time I'd seen Ronnie, he'd been in a staid, conservative business suit, something he wore like a uniform most of the time. I was really happy that Hanna had finally decided to marry him. Though it was ancient history now, I couldn't help but feel special delight at the thought of having my grandson surrogate-parented by a man who'd worked his way through college and earned an accountant's credentials by playing the role of Mickey Mouse at Disney World.

In the next few days we crammed in sights the way tourists do: Plymouth Rock and Plimoth Plantation, complete with realistic recreations of what life was like for the Pilgrims aboard the *Mayflower* and in the establishment of their colony; the New Alchemy Institute, where I'd bought seedlings but never taken time to tour the all-organic agricultural experiment; the free aquarium housed at the Woods Hole Oceanographic Institute; the sand dunes at the Cape's tip; and Provincetown, where New England fisherfolk coexist with artists of every sort in a uniquely diverse atmosphere.

"I think I'll retire and become a beach bum right here," Ronnie said one evening as Arnie sipped at his wine and tugged on his beard. "Imagine being able to spend every day in cut-off jeans and sandals instead of a business suit. And being comfortable without air conditioning. It's almost better than my fantasy about being a Hell's Angel. Can I move into the linen closet with you, Arnie?"

"He's a coo-coo," Arnie said. "You be a good boy."

"Even you, Arnie? There's a plot afoot to keep my free spirit imprisoned in an accountant's body!"

"Good boy, Arnie," Hanna said. "He can't retire

until I do. Then we'll get a farm near here, set it up like New Alchemy, and return to the land."

"I'd go along with that," Ronnie said. "Let's do it."

"Yeeaah!" Travie cheered. "Really, can we move to the Cape? I'm already saving money to buy my favorite house here. You could have all of it if you want to buy a farm instead."

Hanna gave him one of those looks mothers reserve for too-precocious outbursts from their children. "When the mortgage is paid off, and the business loan, and all the zillion other little loans for things like the cars and TVs and the microwave oven and our honeymoon to Peru and your braces and a college education and—probably about the year two thousand fifty."

"Awwwww!" Travie's disappointment was evident, and shared by me. The trouble with the young upwardly mobile professionals is that the more affluent they become, the more traps they set for themselves, leaving no choice but to keep the momentum going. And they're the same generation that invented dropping out as a way of protesting the same tendency in their parents. Well, one brief week had planted the seed of yearning to be free of the trap. Perhaps by the time Hanna and Ronnie left, the yearning would firm up into a commitment for the future. Though it might be selfishness on my part, I plotted to show them such a wonderful time that they would return to Florida eager to get back to New England, and I felt no remorse over the plotting. It's unnatural for families to be separated by enormous distances.

As we were planning a more relaxed second week, Ronnie called his office to check on a project he'd thought could run smoothly without him. As comptroller of an enormous resort complex in Miami, he'd felt the obligation of conscience to make that phone call, but it was a mistake. Something was going wrong; it required his personal touch, and Ronnie had to cut short his vacation. When we put that conservative young businessman in his conservative business suit onto a plane in Hyannis that sunny Sunday, he leaned over and whispered in to my ear, "Tell Arnie to save me a place on that shelf in the closet. My body may be leaving, but my soul is staying here."

Almost as though it had stayed picture-perfect strictly for Ronnie's benefit, the weather turned downright cold and dismal overnight. While I brushed my teeth the next morning, I could hear the mournful lowing of the foghorn at the entrance to Falmouth Harbor. "Let's hope this is just a passing weather front," I said to the two animals who always kept me company for my morning rituals. Bundy quit chewing on the hairbrush he'd taken over for his own morning mouth cleansing and looked at me with eyes that said, *Does this mean you'll quit gadding about and stay home with us for a change today?* Arnie's head popped from behind the towel hanging over the toilet tank top long enough for him to say "Good! You come see me." Then he disappeared behind the towel again and whistled "Mary Had a Little Lamb." Guiltily, I acknowledged that I had been neglecting them lately, but we had planned to go into Boston that day.

"Good morning," Arnie said. "Good morning. How are you? Did you come see me? Good morning!"

"Good morning, Arnie," Hanna's voice said. She peeped around the door leading to the basement rooms she and Travie were sharing. "Good morning, Mumma. We don't have to go into Boston today, do we? Please?"

"Of course not. Did you want to do something else instead?"

"Absolutely. Sleep! I didn't get a wink last night. Either your chimney is haunted or there's a bird nest in it. I thought I heard something moving in there when Ronnie was here, but it didn't keep me awake. Last night it did. Brrrrrr! It's cold. How wonderful!"

"You could make a fire downstairs. That would take the chill off. Oh, wait a minute—if there are birds nesting in the chimney, then they probably still have babies with them."

"No fire. I'd rather snuggle under the covers anyway. It's a delicious feeling I don't get to enjoy in Florida, and that's what I'm going to do now. Good night."

"Night-night, you go to sleep," Arnie said. "Bye-bye. See you later. Night-night, you go to sleep. Bye-bye. See you later." Excitedly, he jumped from the basin countertop to his post behind the towel, over and over again. Bundy gave him a look of contempt and went back to chewing the hairbrush while I finished brushing my teeth. Arnie was like a cheering squad to our efforts as he hopped in and out of hiding, singing and talking all the while.

It was another game he'd taken to playing. Once he flew from the living room on his outings, I was never sure if he would wind up in the linen closet or behind the towel. He lurked for me in one place or the other, occasionally calling out a "Did you come see me?" or a smattering of song, then becoming so quiet I'd wind up going to look for him. When I found him, he pounced out at me, landing on my hand or head or clinging to my shirtfront with a "Hi there" or "Peek-a-boo" before going back into hiding. This morning he seemed to be dancing as he popped in and out of his bathroom hiding place, singing such a constant happy song that it would seem he knew we'd be keeping him company today.

Hanna slept until noon, and Travie quietly watched TV with the animals. After lunch I went downstairs to listen to the fireplace, curious to hear the noises that had kept Hanna awake. Though both fireplaces were vented through the same chimney, I'd been unable to detect a sound from the one upstairs, but I was remembering the way the cats had taken to jumping into it when the ashes were cold a while back. Since the fire screen hadn't been enough to keep them out, I'd bought glass doors that effectively barricaded the hearth, but now I was wondering if their actions and these noises might be connected. I didn't think birds were the culprits; birds don't generally move about much at night.

Travie hunkered beside me as I banged the damper door back and forth. We listened. No sound. I banged the damper again with all the oomph I could give it. Still nothing.

"Whosoever ye be, ye best be gone, Sir Ghost," Travie shouted up the flue. "I'll have my wizard cast a spell upon you, er, upon ye, t'will turn ye into a toad. Hark, Lady Margarete, methinks yon beast be stirring."

I listened. There was a quiet rustling within the upper reaches of the chimney. Soot fell onto the hearth. The rustling became louder. This beastie was no bird. "Squirrels!" I said. "They have enough trees for their nests, but I guess we'd better let them stay, Travie. I don't think their babies are weaned yet. They aren't old enough to be moved."

A shower of soot fell. The rustling noises became a frantic scrabbling, scratching sound. This time, the soot fell in an avalanche that hurled a cloud of ashy dust into our faces. Dismayed, Travie and I looked at each other. His face was caked with black. "Too late," I said. "They're on the move. I only hope they take the babies with them."

"Oohh! You don't think they'll desert them, do you?"

"I don't know. Let's go outside and see what comes out of the chimney."

We raced up the stairs and pelted toward the back door. "What are you doing?" Hanna asked with alarm. "What are you doing" Arnie echoed. "You wanna go outside? Bye-bye. See you later!"

The cats pounded after us, leaping through the door at our heels. We ran across the patio, stopped beneath the oak tree, and looked up. And waited. Nothing emerged from the chimney.

"Look, Margarete," Travie said excitedly and ran onto the porch. "Look at the drainpipe; you painted it white last year, I know, but look at it now!" I looked. The drainpipe was coated with black smudges. "And look up there," he said, pointing at the underside of the gutter. Black smudges were there, too, and three perfect imprints of a critter's paws. They were much too large for a squirrel.

Comprehension dawned. "They wouldn't leave without their babies," I said. "Let's go watch a while longer, Travie." We ran back into the yard. This time Hanna joined us. We waited and watched the chimney and were soon rewarded with the cautious emergence of two fuzzy brown ears, then two black-masked eyes, a button-black nose, and a mouth clutching a squirming mass of fur. "Hello, friend raccoon," I said. "So that's where you've been all winter. Beautiful baby you have there. You

can stay if you want to. So sorry for the distur-
bance."

"Sir Lancelot, there be ye," Travie said. "Fear
not. We will not harm thee."

"I think that's the mother, Travie," Hanna said.

"Lady Guinevere," he corrected, "fear not. I am
one of thy husband's knights. I am pledged to protect thee."

She looked at us, hopped out of the chimney with
a nimble bound, and walked carefully with her burden toward a front corner of the roof. Her babe dangled quietly from her jaws, watching us with bright
curiosity.

"Let's see where they go," Travie whispered
loudly, and he was through the gate and gone before
I could warn him not to cut off the raccoon's escape
route. With Hanna following, I went after him. He
was standing in the middle of the street, where he
could have a good view of the chimney and roof
while allowing the raccoon plenty of space for her
retreat.

As we watched, she carefully placed her burden
in a crotch of one of the evergreen trees that
brushed the roof of the house. The baby clung for
dear life, waiting for his mother to climb around
him to a lower branch, from which vantage point
she grabbed the scruff of his neck and lowered him
to another crotch. After repeating the maneuver all
the way to the ground, the coon mother ran across
the lawn with her baby and began to clamber up
one of the forty-foot spruce trees near the fence line.
Her progression up that tree was marked by the

bending and swaying of branches all the way to the top, where she deposited the little one and started down again. As we watched that afternoon, she moved two more babies from the chimney to the spruce tree. For one brief instant, we were treated to the sight of a little masked face peering at us from the end of one upper branch, then that abruptly disappeared and all movement ceased.

"Are they going to be all right up there?" Travie asked. "They won't fall out or anything, will they?"

"Raccoons are some of the smartest creatures on the face of the earth," I said. "They'll be just fine. Tonight she'll probably go in search of a better home for them to live in until it's time for them to strike out on their own."

"If Lady Guinevere has to house-hunt tonight, she won't have time to find a meal for them, too," Travie said. "Can I put some food under the tree for their supper?" The large bowl of cat food he placed under the tree that evening was empty the next morning. But after an all-day watch, we concluded that the raccoons had gone elsewhere. Though I had great faith in Lady Guinevere's ability to take care of her children, I regretted that we had made them move. They'd been doing no harm, after all, though I shuddered to think of the problems it would have caused had one of them fallen down the chimney and wound up inside the house.

Never a summer goes by on the Cape when the papers don't carry at least one story of such an incident, usually at a home that's empty until the summer months. During the winter or spring, the coons move into what is to them a ready-made, un-used den, then find themselves suddenly displaced by returning human owners. In the course of being forcibly evicted, they frequently find themselves locked inside a house and panic; then, in attempts to escape what is to them a big trap, they cause great damage to human belongings. An upsetting situa-tion for everyone concerned, of course.

Personally, I can't help but side with the animals. It is, after all, we who are taking over their homes. When I'd first moved to my neighborhood, mine had been one of only a handful of houses on the block for years. I'd routinely had deer in the back yard then. Now the deer were gone, and it wouldn't be long, either, before all the others creatures moved on, too. That summer, two of the six wood-ed lots on my street were cleared for houses that would be used only two months of the year by hu-mans from cities who came to the Cape to be closer to nature. And even I was guilty of the inadvertent cruelty of evicting a struggling mother while she was caring for her young. Sadly, I realized that I might never again see Lady Guinevere or any of her kind in my neighborhood.

As far as Travie was concerned , the raccoon in-cident was the most exciting thing that happened on that vacation. Because the weather was unusu-ally cool, foggy, and wet, we stuck close to the house, not doing much of anything. But I think he enjoyed it more than he had any summer in years—since the last time he, his mother, and I had all been together for a long, leisurely visit. His "cherrypittree" shot up more than three feet according to the careful measurements he took, and the thriving garden was a perfect setting for his perpetual "quests." While the cats followed him around as though he were the Pied Piper, Arnie rode on his shoulder, pretending to be a sorcerer-turned-raven.

For Arnie, too, it seemed to be an extra happy summer. When he was in the aviary, seldom as that was, he sang and talked so vigorously that I expected him to wake up any morning with laryngitis from the strain on his vocal cords. Even molting didn't still his voice this year as it had the three summers past, I wondered if he was responding to my own frame of mind.

For I was practically in a state of euphoria. The last remnants of a dark cloud of misfortune that had plagued my life in recent years seemed to be leaving me with blue skies at last. Though the sale of the house in Texas had fallen through, it no longer seemed so important. Among my other prospects for the future, there was that gas well being drilled, and as the well deepened, soil samples continued to show great promise.

"I'm surprised you're not down there, Mumma," Hanna teased. "You always said you were going to bring a rocking chair out to that field and watch every minute of the drilling when they got around to it."

I shrugged. "When I said that, the dream of that oil well was the most important thing in life; it kept me going through many difficulties. Now I've stepped into a new and better-than-ever era." I smiled and started to count my blessings. "I'm totally at home here at last, with not a trace of restlessness left in me. I've made peace with myself, you see. I have my animal kingdom, my friends, my family, company enough so I'm always busy cooking. There's my volunteer work, my garden, and maintenance of this old house to keep me challenged. I think I can quit worrying about you at long last. By the way, I'm very proud of the way you've struggled to success with your business. The publisher has great hopes for Arnie's book. The rascal is already a minor celebrity, you know. Never a day goes by that I don't listen to that silly little starling, look out my window, and feel touched by the wonder of life. I'm so happy that I bubble inside all the time! Sometimes dreams come true in the most unexpected ways. I don't even care if the well comes a gusher or a duster now." Then I grinned. "But I know it's not going to be a duster."

Hanna hugged me. "I'm so happy for you. You deserve it all, you know."

"I don't know that I deserve it, but I'm certainly going to bask in the sun while it's shining. As long as the house in Texas is a headache, there's one little cloud to keep it all from being too perfect. This may sound strange, but that's a comforting thought. I don't trust absolute perfection; it's an open invitation to fatal flaws."

I should have listened to my own words. Perhaps they would have prepared me for what was to come.

17 "What's wrong with him? Oh my, that's the strangest thing I've ever seen a bird do. Is he sick? Do you think my flash bulbs frightened him? He looks like he's having a seizure!"

Arnie's feathers stood out from his body like bristling hair on the back of a mad cat. His beak was wide open, and a string of spittle was spun between his mandibles. His tail feathers were spread into a perfect fan, and his wingtips rotated in little circles to either side of his body. He lay on his belly, leaned his head far over to one side, and slowly closed his eyes. Then he made not another move. A shaft of bright, hot sunshine pierced through the picture window, spotlighting the still starling as though he were an object on display.

"Take a picture," I ordered. "Quick!"

"What's going on?" reporter Paul Stevens asked as Joe Sherman took one photograph after another of Arnie's statuelike pose. "What's wrong with him?"

"Nothing," I said. "He's taking a sunbath. I guess it does look pretty alarming when you don't know what he's doing. He enjoys basking in the sun as much as a cat does."

"Wonderful!" Joe said. "Absolutely wonderful poses. These are going to be some great shots."

Joe was the Sunday editor of the *Brockton Enterprise,* and I suspected he'd come to check on Arnie just to humor his mother. Mrs. Sherman, a close friend of M.A.'s and Marie's, had been hearing about Arnie since we'd arrived in town, at which point she began telling her son what a marvelous story Arnie would make for his newspaper.

It had taken one of those "starling invasions" that make the headlines of some paper every year to persuade Joe that Arnie was worth checking out, though. The starlings had invaded his newsbeat this time. The two men intended to do a tongue-in-cheek interview with Arnie, asking him to explain why the starlings had come in large numbers to Brockton, a city south of Boston. The angle of the story changed abruptly when Arnie talked for them. I don't think they believed he could until they heard it with their own ears.

After they did, Arnie became front page news in Brockton. Written by Paul Stevens and illustrated with Joe Sherman's photos, the story was intended to amuse a reading public that was following with mixed emotions the waging of war by their city and the U.S. government on a flock of ten thousand starlings that chose a local neighborhood for a month's vacation. The birds decided they knew when they weren't wanted and left town just a few days before Arnie won the hearts of many Brockton residents, some of whom had been siding with the starlings throughout the war.

Meanwhile, I was waging my own war, this time against an unidentified enemy that was the most conniving sneak thief I'd ever encountered. Kyle, Travie's best friend, had discovered the first theft while vacationing with his mother, Joanne.

Like Travie, Kyle had grown into new interests this year, and those included gardening and photography. While Joanne painted—her way of spending the perfect vacation—Kyle puttered in the garden with me and stalked the household animals and neighborhood wildlife with his camera. While he was stalking the rascally cardinal, who was helping himself to beans and tomatoes, Kyle spotted the first theft.

"Margarete! Margarete, you have to see this to believe it," he shouted as he ran into the kitchen. "Your corn looks like a peeled banana."

"Hi there. He's coo-coo," Arnie said, dropping the string bean he'd stolen from the basket of harvested produce I was preparing for the freezer.

"My corn," I groaned. "Not my corn! They can have anything else in the garden, but I've waited months for that tiny patch of corn to mature. Arnie, you go home. I have to check this out."

Kyle and I parted our way through the overgrown paths that were beginning to resemble mole holes through a tropical forest. "Too much nitrogen," I muttered. "Too much leafy green stuff. Have to remember that next year."

"You need more phosphate and potassium," Kyle said wisely. "Or maybe just bigger paths. It's a super garden, Margarete."

I put my arm across his shoulders, amazed that he'd already grown as tall as I. "Thanks, pal. Maybe you can help me figure out how to save the corn."

"Da-dum! Here it is," he said with a flourish of his hand. "Isn't that neat?"

Neat? It certainly was. I probably wouldn't have noticed anything amiss if Kyle hadn't spotted it. The stalk stood upright and firmly in the ground, looking virtually untouched. On it, the two ears of corn had been peeled and stripped of every golden kernel. The husks, hanging from the base of each empty cob, indeed looked like dangling banana skins. Nothing else in the patch of corn had been disturbed.

"Travie has a cherrypittree and now you have"— Kyle giggled—"a corncob patch. Sure is a strange garden, Margarete."

"Conniving crows!" I said with a withering look to let him know I didn't appreciate his little witticism. "I've been good to them, too. They're as ungrateful as the squirrels."

"Let's make a scarecrow," Kyle said.

I was willing to try anything. No back-yard garden has room for much corn, so I had carefully and deliberately spaced my plantings to make sure I would have just a few ripe ears each week for a couple of months, and I'd waited with mouth-watering anticipation for those first few to be perfect for picking. Everything else in the garden was so bountiful that I'd inundated friends, family, and neighbors with vegetables, packed my freezer for winter, and handed out fresh produce by the bagful to the first person I spotted at the elderly housing project in town. I truly enjoyed sharing it all, but that corn was to be all mine! The beasties had been allowed their way with me for the last time. At the corn patch, I would draw my boundary lines and fight for my territorial rights!

"Yes, let's make a scarecrow, Kyle," I agreed, and we did. It seemed to work, too. When Kyle and Joanne left a week later to visit her mother in Canada, the corn was still secure, and I was eyeing four ears that would reach the peak of perfection within the next day or two. Then the thief struck again—cleaned all four ears, slick as a whistle, right down to the cob. This time, one of the stalks was tilted toward the ground, leaning as though bowed beneath a weight too heavy for its roots to support.

That's when I really brought in the ammunition. My arsenal of weapons included long poles that I stuck into the ground around the corn patch, suspending from them strips of plastic that flapped in the breeze; wind chimes that were far too musical to frighten anything; aluminum pie plates that banged together in the wind and frightened every single bird from the yard until I took them down; a phony snake and inflatable great horned owl, both guaranteed to keep birds at bay; and my own great, hulking presence in the garden whenever I had time to be out there.

Nothing worked. In six weeks, the only corn I'd tasted from my garden had been green because I'd gotten overanxious and picked it too early. Somehow, the thief always knew when it was at the peak of flavor and beat me to each perfect ear. Finally, I admitted defeat. Jack in the Beanstalk, the town's greengrocer, had local corn that was fresh picked daily, anyway. I bought mine and allowed the crows to have what they'd claimed as theirs.

Only then did I discover that I had been maligning the poor, innocent crows without reason. Awakening in the middle of one night, I looked at the clock and groaned; two-thirty in the morning is an obscene time to be awake. After half an hour of tossing and turning, I was still wide-eyed. Maybe a glass of orange juice would settle me, I decided, and tiptoed to the kitchen.

It was bright as day in there. The full harvest moon was high in the sky, cloaking the world in a silvery sheen. As I poured the orange juice, I heard a high-pitched ti-chitti-chi-che-chee-chee-cheee, ti-chitti-chee-chee coming from the back yard. It was a new sound to me, one that I fancifully imagined might come from tiny alien invaders. Perplexed, I looked out the window. At the back of the yard, four creatures with masked faces stood on their hind legs, drinking from the bird bath.

"So you and your family are still around, Lady Guinevere," I murmured, smiling as I watched. My smile didn't last long. When they'd had their fill of water, Lady Guinevere and her three youngsters lined up single file and pranced across the lawn to the garden, straight to the corn patch. By the light of the moon, I could see very clearly as she carefully sniffed at first one stalk, then another, until she found just the right one. She reached up and grasped it between her front paws, bent it toward the ground, and held it in position as two of her kits carefully peeled an ear. Then they took turns nibbling.

"So now we know who my corn culprits are," I told Patsy the next day.

"Isn't it wonderful, Margarete"—she laughed— "even in the middle of the night, you're never without company at your house."

"I don't know how wonderful it is." I sighed. "Sometimes I think the animal kingdom around here is too much company."

"Nonsense! Think how dull your life would be without them. Each day those animals bring you some new excitement."

A phone call from Paul Stevens in Brockton later in the week made me remember Patsy's words. His message made me think the excitement was only beginning. "Mrs. Corbo, I just got a phone call from Hollywood, California, about your little Arnie. It seems that one of our readers clipped that

272

story I wrote about him and sent it to the producers of the television show 'That's Incredible.' They may want to do a segment on Arnie for their show. They'll be calling you personally later today."

I kept my telephone lines clear that day, giving hasty explanations to friends who called, and asking them to hang up. As the hours rolled by, my excitement diminished. At eight o'clock, which made it five o'clock in Hollywood, I gave up on the call ever coming. "It was probably just a practical joker," I said to Arnie. "Maybe they'll still call, though. Who knows what kind of hours those show business people keep. Do you want to stay up with me and wait a while longer, Arnie? I was hoping you might say a few words while they were on the phone."

He gave me a cranky look, said "Night-night, you go to sleep," and went back to picking at his toes with his beak, a strange new habit he'd acquired. I took his hint, turned off the bright lights, and covered him for the night.

Early the next morning I answered the phone to hear a voice say, "Mrs. Corbo, this is John Kirk calling from 'That's Incredible.'" It was only a tentative proposition, he explained, but his boss, Shelly Rosen, thought that Arnie had marvelous possibilities as a segment on one of their shows for the coming year. They had to submit all story ideas to a production board for approval, however, before they could begin to work on a project. Could I send them newspaper clippings, tapes of Arnie talking, any kind of material that would help them make an effective presentation before the board?

"Of course," I said. "I'll get a package to you by next week." I was beginning to be an old hand at accepting with aplomb the fact that interest in the wonder of Arnie, the talking starling, was spreading like the ripples created by a pebble tossed into a pond.

It wasn't until I hung up the telephone, however, that it hit me. This was no pebble in a pond. It was more like a meteor plunging into the ocean. "That's Incredible" was a national prime-time television program. It was watched by millions of people every Monday night. *Millions* of people. That was awesome to contemplate. I sat back in my chair and lit a cigarette, toying with the idea of sending a polite note saying "Thank you for considering us, but no thank you." I honestly didn't know if I wanted Arnie to become *that* famous.

A strange dread was growing in me. There were times when I wished I could take us back to the first days of our arrival in Falmouth, that I could then do everything over again but without opening my big mouth so much to spread the word about the treasure that was mine.

I liked the simple life we had, the love and warmth that permeated my household, and really didn't want to have it disrupted—not for fame, not for fortune, not for any imaginable tradeoff. But then, maybe my little darling's story belonged to the world. In his own small way, perhaps he could make it a better place to live for us all, and possibly, by opening the eyes of people who'd disliked his kind without knowing much about them, he'd make a better world for starlings.

I could accept it all with more ease, I felt certain, if only his presence in my life hadn't begun to make me feel that he was . . . that he was a good luck charm! For as Arnie's notoriety increased, so did my personal good fortune.

The house in Texas was leased by a couple who kept horses. They said they'd probably ask for an option to buy it after they'd lived there long enough to be certain it was the right place for them. Their monthly rent didn't even cover the mortgage, but I didn't care—it was being lived in again. It had always made me sad to think of that house empty after I'd poured so much love into the creation of it. Almost simultaneously, news came that the drilling crew had hit pay dirt with the well. It would have to be capped until there was a pipeline to carry the gas to market, and that would take another year or so, but there it was, my dream come true; I had a part interest in a well that the oil people called "a good producer." Plans were being firmed up for the publication of Arnie's book and, already, words like *classic* were being attached to it. I was content, more optimistic, *happier* than I'd ever been in my life.

"You're so lucky," Chrissie kept saying. As a matter of fact, many people were saying that, little knowing the heart, soul, blood, sweat, tears, and toil that had been poured into making the luck happen. I couldn't blame them. Even I felt that luck was a great part of every success story. And I don't trust luck any more than I trust perfection.

"I don't like it," I said to Patsy. "It's all too good to be true. The piper has to be paid somewhere along the line."

"You've already paid the piper," she said. "Relax and enjoy it, Margarete."

"It's too much good luck all at once," I said to M.A.

"I'll trade places with you any time you want, Maa-gret," she said.

"Mama would be lighting candles to ward off the evil that's sure to follow," I said to Dieter.

"My sister, the doubter," he said. "Our mother enjoyed her little superstitions, but that's all they were."

"It scares me," I said to April. "Something is bound to go wrong."

"I know exactly how you feel, dear," she said. "But I think you've earned some good times."

"What do you think?" I asked Diane. "Am I just being a silly fool to worry so much?"

She didn't answer right away, but then, Diane likes to weigh the time of day before declaring it. Finally she said, "If fate has anything to do with karmic debt, then it must be balanced by karmic credit. That would explain good and bad luck. Maybe your debt is paid and it's time for you to collect the credit owing to you. All is well with your world. Quit worrying!"

"You're right," I said. "All is well with my world, and that's exactly what has me worried."

"You're getting peculiar, Margarete," she said. "Better watch that or you'll wind up a genuine New

England eccentric."

Maybe I was getting peculiar. Maybe the animals were driving me to it. I'd no sooner nursed Bundy through a badly infected paw—and I suspected a squirrel bite had caused it—than Samantha began throwing up every time she ate, usually on the white carpet. Once Sammie was healed, Mitzi developed a high fever and I almost lost her before the antibiotics took effect. Now she had coughing fits whenever she overexerted herself, so I suspected her old heart was giving out on her. Then Bundy brought me a chipmunk with a big gash on its thigh—it was impossible to know if Bundy had caused the gash or just been able to catch the chipmunk because of it—and I'd nursed that one back to health, a favor he returned by taking over one of my gutter drainpipes and stuffing it so full of what I supposed to be winter stores that the next heavy rain overflowed the clogged gutter and drained down the living room wall. For some strange reason, birds had routinely begun to fly into my picture window and break their necks, and I couldn't seem to hang enough objects in the glass to warn them away. Some disease was killing the local blue jays, and it was killing me to watch how valiantly the ones in my yard struggled to live in the days it took them to die. Worried that it might be something Arnie could catch, I closed the living room windows even on hot days in case it was an airborne bug and faithfully removed my shoes at the door after being in the yard lest it walk in with me.

That was all behind me now, though, and maybe

it had all been part of the piper's price. Perhaps I had simply grown into the time of my life when all was meant to be well in my world. As everyone who knows me well realizes, worrying is one of my favorite hobbies. Surely, indulging that hobby was all that was causing the anxiety in me.

"What do you think, Arnie?" I said. "I seem to have asked everyone except you, and it's your future we're talking about more than mine. We'll need to make a better quality tape recording than any we have for 'That's Incredible,' you know. Should we do it, or just forget the whole thing?"

He quit picking at his toes and looked at me. "I love you, yes I do," he said. "Let's go to work."

18 "I love . . . Did you . . . ? Good . . . You got to . . . "

"What's gotten into you, Arnie?" I said. "You never finish a sentence anymore."

He looked at me without comment, then flew against the door of his aviary and hung onto the screening.

"I'm sorry," I said. "but you know I go swimming with the Easter Seal kids on Tuesday, and I'm running late now. You'll have to wait until I come back for your outing."

I was tired and tempted to use any excuse, even Arnie, to cancel out today, but it was a commitment and people were counting on me. The one-hour-a-week swimming session sponsored by the Easter Seal Society was the only entertainment some of the special kids got, and they were short on volunteers this year. Eddie, who'd been stricken by a rare disease that left him brain damaged, was my *special* special kid, and I just couldn't disappoint him. Only a couple of years older than Travie, Eddie made me realize how fortunate most of us are that our children survive childhood intact.

As I gathered my things, the three cats stared at me with sad disappointment while Arnie pecked frantically at his screening. I hadn't been home much at all lately, and they were all pouting, which was probably why Arnie wasn't talking properly. I'd spoiled them all, and they resented my being gone so much.

Well, it couldn't be helped. It had been a strange and hectic month all the way around. First, Martha's father had been put into intensive care with final-stage cancer; then Martha was admitted with the same stomach problems that had had her in and out of the hospital all year; and Marie had a stroke and died after three days without regaining consciousness; then Martha's father died. Even Ryan died; the big Irish wolfhound had been, technically, Fritz's dog, but Patsy's son lived in the downstairs apartment at her house, and Ryan had spent a great deal of time with her, so he'd left quite a large empty spot in that household. Surrounded by human gloom and doom, I'd had neither time nor patience for my animals lately.

No matter how much loved, pets have to take a

back seat to human needs sometimes. "I'm sorry," I said to mine, "but I really do have to leave you alone one more time. Tomorrow I'll be home all day, I promise." I snatched my keys off the coffee table and stopped in front of the aviary. "You be a good boy while I'm gone, Arnie. C'mere, gimme a kiss."

He hopped down a couple of perches to the one nearest my face and opened his mouth into the biggest yawn imaginable. "Am I boring you?" I laughed.

"Kissy," he said and stuck his beak through a hole that had been poked in the screening during our move. I gave him a quick peck and was off and running.

It wasn't until the next day that I saw enough of Arnie to notice that he wasn't behaving normally in several little ways. He yawned a lot, for one thing . . . or was he yawning? There was something strange about the way he opened his beak that reminded me of the way humans open their mouths for a heartfelt "Oooucchh," and he seemed to do it only when he moved from one perch to another. Come to think of it, he was sliding down that ladder of perches these days instead of hopping steadily as he'd always done. And he had that new habit of picking at his toes.

I sighed. "Arnie, I have a feeling that you've picked up a splinter, little boy. Much as we both hate it, I'm going to have to catch you so I can get a good look."

He looked at me as though to say, *Well, it's about*

time you noticed! Then he grabbed his ankle between his mandibles and lifted his foot so high he could have wrapped it around his neck. It looked remarkably as though he was trying to get it into position so he could scrutinize it himself.

I opened the door to the aviary. "C'mon out here, Arnie. Let's get this ordeal over with." He hesitated, eyeing me suspiciously.

Trying to catch him was always a challenge requiring subterfuge, speed, and downright sneakiness. Actually capturing him was an art at which I was but a bumbling amateur. The two or three times a year I'd been forced to do so in order to trim his nails and beak had always required hours, sometimes days, of elaborate game-playing before I could emerge the winner. I hated the necessity for insulting his sense of dignity as much as he hated being hand held, but it was part of the price for our unlikely alliance.

"Well, suit yourself," I said, turning my back to him and walking away.

He flew to my shoulder and whistled a few bars of Beethoven's Fifth, then snuggled against the hair at the nape of my neck. "Let's see what's in the news today," I said and sat down with the newspaper in hand. As soon as I opened the pages, he hopped to my left wrist and pecked at the paper. Slowly, ever so slowly, I lowered it to my lap, raised my right hand, scratched my nose with it, then snatched—my left wrist.

Arnie sat on my foot and trrrrpppped. "You be a good boy!" he said, took to the air with a chortle, flew down the hallway, and made a sharp right turn into the bathroom. I sat for a while, allowing him to think I'd given up. When he could stand the wait no longer, he summoned me to play with a "Peek-a-boo, peek-a-boo, peek-a-boo. I see you. I love you, yes I do. C'mere, gimme kissy."

"You seem to talk just fine when you want to, obstinate Arnie," I said. Nonchalantly as possible, I closed the bathroom door behind me and ran water from the faucet. Leaning over, I looked at him crouching behind the towel. "Peek-a-boo," he said and pranced cockily onto the countertop.

"You want a drinky?" I asked, letting water run into my cupped hand. Keeping one eye on me, he jumped onto my forearm, sidled to my wrist, perched on my thumb, and leaned down to scoop water into his beak. I let him tilt his head back, swallow it, and lean down for another scoop before my hand swooped down at him and captured—my own thumb. I sighed as he scolded me from behind the towel.

"Smart aleck bird," I said. "Don't you realize that if you have a splinter hurting your foot I can make it well again?" He smirked at me from the opposite end of the tunnel he'd trampled into shape behind the towel—*the perfect trap he'd created for himself*, I suddenly realized. Slowly, I eased my right hand, palm up, behind the towel and toward him. He charged toward me, hopped onto my fingers, and launched into a soulful version of "Mary Had a Little Lamb." I used my left hand to grab the towel, imprisoning Arnie inside. Cupping the fingers of my right hand, I grasped him firmly, brought him out into the light, flipped him onto his back—and gasped.

This was no little splinter with which I had to contend. The bottoms of both his feet had enormous, pus-filled blisters covering at least three quarters of the pads. Remembering how he slid from perch to perch, I wondered if that was the cause of the blisters or if he'd been doing it because it was easier on his feet than hopping. No wonder his mouth flew open in a grimace of pain when he jumped from one wooden stick to another!

"Ooh, Arnie, I'm so sorry, little boy," I said with tears in my eyes. "I should have noticed you were having a problem before this. Don't you worry. I'm going to make your feet well again."

He kicked and twisted and squirmed in my hand, glaring at me with a defiant look that clearly said *Unhand me, you big, overbearing brute! Take your sympathy and your nursing skills and look for another patient.* Beneath my fingers, his heart pounded as though he'd just finished running the Falmouth Road Race.

If his heart pounded that way just because *I* held him, the thought of how severely it might react to a stranger was terrifying. He'd have to have something much more serious than blisters before I'd risk taking him to a vet. "Well, Margarete, you've handled worse situations than this before," I murmured. "Calm down and think!" The pus had to be drained, of course. I sterilized a needle with fire, dunked it into alcohol, then pricked each blister.

Applying gentle pressure, I drained the injuries, painted both feet with mercurochrome, blew it dry, and turned Arnie loose.

From the safety of a curtain rod, he scolded me nonstop for the next five minutes, reverting to the starling sounds he always regarded as more potent than human words for expressing anger and indignation. He bent over, looked at one foot, then the other, giving each the closest scrutiny imaginable— and flew to my shoulder. "I love you," he said. "C'mere, gimme a kiss, bad boy."

"I love you, too, little one. Now let's make your cage more comfortable for those poor feet." I removed the wooden dowels that were his perches. He flew to the lamp and scolded me again. "I'm sorry," I said, "but this is necessary. I wish I could persuade you to sit or lie down or stand on your head or assume any position to get you off your feet for a few days, Arnie, but all of that's impossible for a bird. So I'm going to replace these hard old sticks with some nice flat, padded perches. You'll love them."

I put his food and water on the kitchen table and allowed him to fly free while I fashioned new perches from parts of the ruined shutters I'd removed from the windows. I padded each one with thin foam rubber and wrapped them with pieces of thick white towel. Once I'd drilled new holes into the perch supports to accommodate the larger dowels already in the pieces I was using, Arnie's new furniture would be all set.

He flew to my shoulder frequently to check on

what I was doing, but the novelty of the extended outing soon wore thin. Obviously perplexed when he flew to his cage and found no place to land, he hovered in the doorway as long as he could, then turned in midair and came back to my shoulder. "You go home?" he complained in my ear.

"Soon you can go home," I said. Placing the new perches, I positioned them so far apart that he'd have to use his wings to get from one to the other, thus landing lighter on his feet than he did when jumping. Very proud of my handiwork, I walked to the aviary with Arnie on my wrist, bragging to him. "You're going to be so much more comfortable now, Arnie. I should have thought to do this sooner. Who wants to stand on a hard stick all day, anyway, huh? You're really, really going to love your new perches."

He took one look at them, screeched at the top of his lungs, flew into the hallway, and disappeared. No amount of enticing would persuade Arnie to go into his aviary that day. He spent the night in the linen closet. "I think the discipline around this household is slipping," I grumbled to the cats that night as I closed the bedroom door, a precaution to make certain they wouldn't decide to have a slumber party with Arnie while I was sleeping.

Repeating the towel trick the next morning, I checked his feet. The mercurochrome had rubbed off, I hoped I was mistaken, but it looked as though the pus had begun to form again. Opting for a moderate approach, I decided to wait another day to be certain and painted on more mercurochrome.

While I had him in hand, I carried him to the aviary and locked him in. Like it or not, he was going to have to get used to the new perches, because he wasn't getting the old ones back.

When I captured him the next morning, his feet were festered again. The simple home remedy I'd tried wasn't working. I picked up the phone and called the vet, describing the problem and explaining that Arnie was not accustomed to being handled. "Could I come by to get some antibiotic salve?" I asked. There was a long pause on the other end of the line, then, "You really should bring him in so we can get a look-see. We hate to make a diagnosis and prescribe treatment without seeing a patient."

Reluctantly, I waylaid Arnie behind the towel once again and thrust him into a tiny cage that I hoped would enable me to catch him once we got to the vet's office. Squawking and beating against the imprisoning walls all the way, he made me feel that I was betraying him in some terrible way. Hearing a dog bark inside the waiting room, he threw such a fit, throwing himself from one side of the cage to another, that I really feared the trauma of the strange experience was going to kill him.

The examination was anticlimactic after that. As I held him, the vet took a quick look at his feet and legs, excused himself for almost a quarter hour, then returned with the pronouncement, "Your bird has gout. Stay away from those feet. Gout is a very painful disease already without putting him through any more. Sometimes oral antibiotics will clear it up for a time, but the prognosis isn't very good. You might want to consider euthanasia."

I took the antibiotics, paid the bill, and drove off in a daze. *Consider euthanasia? Put Arnie to sleep— kill Arnie? No, no, the vet had to be mistaken. He had to be!* I'd get a second opinion before I'd consider having Arnie put to sleep.

The second vet did the same disappearing act, then returned with the name of another disease, bumblefoot. It came from repeated trauma to the feet, which happens when a bird lands time after time on a hard or abrasive surface. Oral antibiotics was again the prescription.

"Well, Arnie," I said as we sat together that evening, "looks as if it's up to you and me, kid. Whether you like it or not, I'm going to have to capture you twice a day for a while and somehow persuade you to open your beak long enough to get two drops of medication down your throat."

"He's a little bitty baby boy," he said desultorily. "Love Arnie."

We wrestled twice a day after that, but between our bouts, Arnie seemed to grow ever more cheerful, singing almost nonstop, cuddling up to me when I was idle, as though telling me that he wasn't holding a grudge. Neither was he intending to make my job any easier, though. Every now and then, I honestly did think about euthanasia, but then realized that I was considering it to ease my pain rather than Arnie's. In my upset over his ailment, most of the rest of my life had come to a standstill. I couldn't even leave him alone at home without feeling guilty about it.

My guilt had only begun to grow, however. As I paid my bill at the Grain Mill, I was telling the friendly proprietors about Arnie's and my ordeal when one of the employees interjected, "Bet you had him sitting on those foolish sticks like you see in store-bought birdcages, huh?" Then Frank, who was in charge of the aviaries at the feed and grain store, informed me that wooden dowels are the un-healthiest perches ever invented for most birds, es-pecially if they're unyielding and all the same size. "Just think about their natural habitat," he said. "Tree branches are all different sizes and have a lot of give to them so a bird in nature never has a jar-ring landing. Then we take 'em, stick 'em in cages, and use those hard wooden sticks because they're easy for us to clean. Fine for some birds, but not for one like Arnie. Maybe he has gout, but I'm will-ing to bet on bumblefoot." And I had been so proud of my ingenuity when I'd made him that ladderlike contraption consisting of wooden dowels, all the same size and not very yielding.

"I'll make it up to you somehow, Arnie," I prom-ised as I struggled to pry open his beak and give him his second dose of medication that evening.

Paul Stevens called to ask if I had heard from the people at "That's Incredible." "Do you know, I for-got all about it. I sent the package they asked for, but haven't heard from them. To tell you the truth, it's not very important right now." Then I told him about Arnie. "Do you mind if I write a story about it?" he asked. "We had a lot of phone calls and letters from our readers after that piece I did on Arnie, and I'm certain they'll be interested in this."

This time, a great many of his readers called me directly. I was amazed at the outpourings of sympathy from so many wonderful people. Many of them had treated similar ailments in birds and had advice to give. "The vets really don't know much about treating birds" was a frequent comment. "It's not their fault. Birds have a nasty habit of dying before their owners even know they're sick, so most vets don't see sick birds enough to learn to diagnose and treat them. If you plan to keep birds for pets, you'd better learn as much as you can on your own."

It was all very bewildering. I didn't plan to keep birds. I just wanted to heal Arnie's feet. They were not improving. I went back to the first vet for a refill of the antibiotics. His relief was on duty that day and advised me to increase the medication to three times a day. He confessed that he didn't know much about treating birds, said it was true that most vets don't, that there aren't even many medications that are safe for birds. Things that will heal dogs and cats can kill birds. He said I was doing all that could be done for Arnie.

The holidays came and went without causing more than a tiny ripple in my life. Days and weeks came and went like the flipping of calendar pages, so quickly and so uneventfully that the entire month of January seemed to consist of no more than a handful of days. I was consumed by worry about Arnie. Sometimes it looked as if he was healing, then the infection would flare up again. I consulted other vets to no avail. All agreed the antibiotics were his only hope and that I should continue giving him the medication; most of them recommended euthanasia. In desperation, I ordered my own books on bird medicine, determined to find an answer.

Dorothy O'Brien of Plymouth, one of the people who'd called me with advice, had told me of a method she used for treating bumblefoot on ducks in her neighborhood. Using a modification of her technique, I began to pack Arnie's wounds with a medicated salve.

Then someone recommended Dr. Margaret Petrak, a veterinarian who specialized in birds, at Boston's Angell Memorial Hospital. At last! An expert in bird medicine. I made an appointment with her. On the morning of the appointment, the worst snowstorm of the season was in full swing; roads to Boston were closed.

"Oh, Arnie, this is so unreal!" I wailed as together we watched the snow fall. "You've been so healthy most of your life. Am I doing the wrong thing? Are you in pain? Am I being cruel by allowing you to live?"

He rubbed his head against my cheek. "You're a coo-coo," he said. "I love you, yes I do." In truth, he no longer seemed to be in pain. He chattered cheerfully from sunup to sundown, giving the house a downright festive air. Had I become a secondhand hypochondriac over Arnie? How could I keep our lives so upset over a health problem with a silly name like bumblefoot? Was it only my imagination that the color seemed to be draining from his skin, his legs, the inside of his mouth, as though he had acquired anemia?

By then, some of the medical books I'd ordered had come in and I'd begun to read. There were little references here and there to the dangerous side effects that go hand in hand with "indiscriminate use of antibiotics." Now I worried that I'd been overdosing Arnie; he had, after all, been on that medication for almost three months. Acting on my own instinct, I quit giving it to him and scheduled another appointment with Dr. Petrak. She had sounded so genuinely concerned and caring when I'd talked with her on the phone that I really wanted her to take a look at him. Meanwhile, I continued to wrestle with Arnie several times a day so I could pack those nasty sores with the ointment.

His feet finally began to heal. At first I thought it was my wishful imagination, but within days I was certain that the abscesses on his feet were shrinking. I crossed my fingers and kept using the medicated salve.

The day of the appointment with Dr. Petrak dawned bleak and dreary. It was snowing again, though lightly so far, and the roads were icy. And Arnie's feet were completely healed! I was wishy-washy about putting him through that long trip to Boston. Now, though, I was worried about his anemic appearance and concerned about the damage that might have been caused by the antibiotics. When I noticed two tiny flecks of dried blood on one of his legs, I decided my peace of mind was worth the trip.

"I hope this will be the last time we have to go through this, Arnie," I said as I caught him behind the towel.

"You be nice! C'mere, gimme a kiss. I love you," he said.

Suddenly, there was blood on my hands. "What on earth . . . ?" Fresh and warm, the blood gushed from Arnie's upper leg. Quickly,, I clamped my thumb over the wound, put my forefinger on the other side of his leg, and squeezed hard until the flow stopped. "Oh, no, Arnie. Not now. Your feet are well! What on earth is happening here?"

His expression was one of complete bewilderment. He didn't understand what was happening any more than I did. I yelled for Diane, who'd agreed to make the trip to Boston with me. "Call the vet and ask him to meet me at his office. Tell him Arnie's bleeding to death!" It was six-twenty in the morning, but the veterinarian's answering service called him at home and he phoned us back. While I applied pressure to Arnie's leg, he talked to Diane. "Use an ice cube and give it time. The bleeding will stop."

It slowed down, but forty-five minutes later blood was still leaking gently past my thumb. "Keep the ice fresh. Keep the pressure constant. You have to give it time," the vet said. "If that doesn't do the trick, I'll meet you at my office."

Diane called Dr. Petrak, who was already at work at Angell Memorial. "It'll take you two hours to get here," she reminded gently. "If he continues to bleed . . . well, birds are small creatures. They can't afford to lose much blood." We drove to my vet's office and barged through the door like maniacs. "It's an emergency!" I yelled to the woman behind the desk. "Arnie's bleeding to death!" A woman sitting in the waiting room with her dog looked bewildered. When the dog barked, Arnie squirmed for the first time since I'd grabbed him in that desperate grip. "It's the doctor's day off," the receptionist said, "and his assistant hasn't arrived yet."

"It's a life and death situation," Diane yelled. "Wait in the treatment room," the receptionist said and reached for the telephone. When the doctor arrived, I had to pry my thumb loose so he could look at the wound. The bleeding had slowed to a thin trickle. The styptic powder he sprinkled on it stopped the blood flow entirely. I quit holding my breath. "Take him home and feed him liver to build up his strength again." The vet smiled.

I shoved pieces of liver down Arnie's throat for the next hour or so. Too weak to stand, he didn't struggle, didn't make a sound. His eyes never left mine, the expression on his face changing from indignation to pleading to bewilderment to resignation as his body grew steadily colder. Finally, he couldn't even swallow. "Okay, little boy, no more torture," I said. I held him to me as tears rolled uncontrollably down my cheeks. He tilted his beak up so he could see me, then rested his head on my breast.

Numbly, I sat there for the next hour cuddling

him. Gently as a feather floating on a breeze, the life force that had been Arnie ebbed from the little bird body that I clutched in my hands. Finally, he struggled to lift his head, looked up at me with love light shining in his eyes, and breathed a tired sigh. It was his final breath.

The ground was frozen. As I'd done once before with another bird, I put his body in the middle of a flower pot filled with dirt. I would bury him in the spring, when the ground thawed and his kind had begun to make new little starlings. I wondered if there was such a thing as reincarnation for birds.

"I feel as though I killed him," I said to Diane as we shared a glass of wine for lunch. For the first time in weeks, I wished I had a cigarette. Almost with a sense of offering a sacrifice in exchange for his life, I had quit the nasty habit during Arnie's illness.

Diane looked at me through her own red-rimmed eyes. "You didn't kill Arnie, Margarete. Ignorance did. I ran across a reference in one of those books you ordered that said prolonged antibiotic use can destroy the blood's ability to clot. You know, Arnie was a starling. No one knows much about them. Maybe they don't respond to the same antibiotics as other birds."

She paused for a long while, then said softly, "Or maybe it was just time for him to go. Maybe because Arnie has fulfilled his purpose in this world."

19 Snow squeaked beneath my boots, I trudged a path become so familiar that it was no longer necessary to watch where I was going. Hands deep in jacket pockets, collar upturned to my nose, ski cap pulled to my eyebrows, I walked with head down, watching sparkling ice crystals crush beneath my feet. Untrodden snow shining beneath the winter sun is so clean, so pure, that it makes one feel newly born into an unpopulated world. Even my footprints, trailing behind me, could not despoil the beauty of winter after a blizzard. Though perhaps my thoughts could, gloomy, dark, and brooding as they were. Only when I had mounted the hill did I stop to look about me. And remember, as always, the first day, when I'd parked the Blazer and rental trailer on this spot before driving the last few blocks, a minor pause so I could revel in being home again.

The gray Atlantic had glowered then, its surface waters whipped to frothy white peaks by a stiff south wind. Deeply resonant, the channel marker buoys clanged notice of their presence to the incoming vessel. Like a wraith, the *Island Queen* materialized slowly out of the mist, her prow aimed at the harbor entrance, her point of embarkation a barely visible smudge on the horizon behind her. In the distance, the Nobska Point lighthouse seemed to float among clouds. Ducks and gulls bobbed near the jetties, sparrows and starlings lined the white fence barricading the bluff dropoff. Picture postcard, I'd thought, then remembered that picture postcards seldom show scenes without sun and never reflect the changes that make the same view new from day to day. I had come for the changes.

In the course of individual human events, we all come to a crossroad where the past beckons like life's most brightly shining star while the future appears dark, uninviting, devoid of promise or purpose. Then we yearn to grab hold of what has been, to hold it before us as a shield against what we fear may or may not be. "Midlife crisis" is one apt description, though the condition has been known to strike at any time between the ages of twelve and a hundred.

At the climax of my midlife crisis, I'd packed the bird, the cats, and all my belongings and sought the refuge of humans since time immemorial—home. Though I'd been doubtful it could ever again be home to me, I was determined to sort out my life.

"Time will tell if I stay, but I got us here, gang," I'd said as I stared through the windshield of the car "Good! I love you. Gimme a kiss," the raspy bird voice had said from the back seat.

Trust Arnie to know exactly the right words to make me feel I'd done something wonderful. He'd always been great for my ego. It seemed we'd always been together, perhaps because he had been with me, serving as confidant, loving me, helping me to stay strong, through a difficult period of time. Friends are like that, though—always there when it counts. It doesn't balance out, however, if they're not around to share the good times, too. I sighed raggedly. How I missed that raspy little voice. I'd never walked so much in my life as I was doing these days, escaping the house that was suddenly so silent no matter how loud the radio or television.

With one more sweeping glance, I took in the nearness of the Vineyard and Nobska on this day when the water was like a gigantic brooch, emerald green studded with countless sparkling sun diamonds. Two lovers embraced atop a jetty ringed with an ice plate that blurred about the edges. Meltdown had begun, and the ice would soon be gone, as would the snow currently occupying the summertime place of bronzed human bodies atop the sand.

Changing, ever changing, that scene, the one constant being the birds to whom it all belonged.

I'd found the changes I'd sought and much more, of course. Now it was up to me to keep change happening, for that's the way the human spirit grows, especially if it has roots, the constant of a home.

I bowed my head and walked down the hill, past boarded-up summer houses and hotels, along the shore, and around the curve to the pond. A lone man shooshed toward me on cross-country skis, misty breath preceding the red cheeks and chapped lips with which he smiled a greeting as we passed. I smiled back, welcoming his presence as a reminder that I was not alone, though I'd chosen to be these past weeks. Arnie's death might be trivial compared to the losses of Martha, her father; M.A., her mother; Patsy and April, their sons. But still, there was emptiness in all those spaces Arnie had occupied in my days. Fritzi, still missing his dog, knew.

Rounding the pond's shoreline, I stepped off the road into a clearing for the ritual that now filled one of those empty spaces. Within seconds the first green-headed mallard flew toward me, honking to his fellows to follow. His wings angled down, his webbed feet spread and pointed forward as he braked for a landing. Hitting the ice, he skidded with flailing wings and wobbling body for several yards before sliding into the water. Surely he could have landed less jarringly on the water surface, as most of the others were doing, but some of them always took that ice slide route. They paddled toward me and waddled to my feet as I scattered cracked corn on snow muddied by myriad footprints, mute testimony that others also fed the ducks here.

Starlings fluttered to the ground and stood nearby, waiting for the leavings. "Bet nobody feeds you guys," I said and tossed them bread from another bag. When they'd finished, the ducks swam off and the starlings jumped into the pond's edge for a bath.

"Starlings, starlings, everywhere, but not an Arnie for Margarete," I mumbled as I resumed the walk home.

And so they did seem to be everywhere these days. Probably they always had been, but I'd failed to notice the fact until a very special one had come into my life. It made me muse about how many other little touches of wonder I'd missed along my way and how much richer could have been my experience if I'd taken time all along to observe what came into my line of sight. Funny how we can do that, looking straight through without noticing them in our preoccupied existences. Because of Arnie, I had learned to see, rather than merely look at, the world around me, and in doing so had gained an acuteness of vision as wondrous as the discovery of color where once had been only black and white. As I thought it, I lifted my eyes from the ground and looked to the trees, so alive with activity. "Don't ever again forget to look," I chided myself.

Arriving home, I rushed to close the door and cross the room. Entering the house without being greeted by a "Hi there" was almost as difficult as making it all the way from my bedroom to the coffeepot each day without benefit of a "Good morning." I tossed my coat and cap on the couch, grabbed a book, and settled down to get lost in its pages.

Sammie bounced from the floor and curled up in the middle of my reading material. Bundy nipped my heel, meowed, and ran to Mitzi's side. She was in the kitchen, looking pointedly at their empty food dishes. There was a tap on the window glass, and I glanced up to see Manx dangling upside down, staring at me. On a jutting branch of one Christmas tree, a blue jay glared in, opened his mouth, and screeched. Mourning doves stood shoulder to shoulder along the telephone line in front of the house, and the branches of the corner oak tree were laden with starlings, sparrows, crows, and the pair of ravens who'd recently joined my soup line. The male cardinal perched precariously on the tip of an upright lilac branch, and I knew his mate wouldn't be far away. Like a theater crowd, they all looked in one direction—at me.

An astrologer in Florida had once informed me that I was born to a life of service. Trudi warned that I would feel fulfilled only if I kept that fact always in mind. I'd thought she meant service to mankind. It had never occurred to me that my services would include being chief cook, bottle washer, and waitress for the local wild kingdom!

I looked at them all and sighed. "I take it none of you wants me to read, and I guess it must be feeding time at the zoo." Then I laughed, for I was not alone and probably never would be again as long as I lived. And, of course, it wasn't fitting that I mark Arnie's passing by going back to the depressed state of mind in which he'd found me. "Shame on you, Margarete," I said for him.

I dished out double portions of cat food, sunflower seeds and mixed birdseed for all the creatures furred and feathered, then tossed half a loaf of bread into the yard. Sooner or later it would all be eaten by one creature or another. Digging in the freezer, I located a hunk of fat, ran a straightened clothes hanger through its middle, and hung it in the spruce tree for the flicker and downy woodpeckers, who'd doubtless be joined by most of the other birds in nibbling at it for days to come. Then I filled the bird bath, knowing it would be well used before I had to empty it to prevent freezing. Starlings were the first to take advantage of the water, as usual.

Watching them bathe and squabble over whose turn it was, I picked up the telephone and started to make calls I'd been neglecting; "Hi, Patsy, how about stopping by for lunch tomorrow?" "Martha, why don't we meet downtown for coffee in a couple of hours?" "M.A., I'm going shopping. Why don't you join me?" "Zelda, I'm available for the Easter Seal program again. When's the next swim?" "April, just wanted to see how you're doing." "Dieter, I'm making cauliflower soup tonight. Maybe you'd like to pick some up on your way home." "Hanna, how about sending Travie for spring vacation again this year?"

The next morning I dismantled the aviary, put it into the basement, and rearranged the furniture.

I moved the bird bath closer to the house so I

could see it better. In my little bit of idle time, I watched the birds more carefully than ever. Amazing how many baths starlings take in one day. Incredible that I'd never noticed them before when their behavior pattern is so unique. How much like Arnie they all acted—regular clowns compared to the other birds. Gee, had the house always been so quiet before he'd arrived to fill it with his song and chatter? How had I ever endured such silence? But, of course, I would soon grow accustomed to it again. Wouldn't I?

When Edelweiss and Lady Guinevere began to appear again, I took the flower pot from the ash can, chopped a deep hole into the almost-thawed earth, and dumped the entire contents of the pot into it. Just a bird's body maybe, but it had been occupied by Arnie's spirit and deserved a safe place in my yard. Atop the spot I planted a clump of crocuses salvaged by the bulldozer driver who cleared the lot across the street from April's house.

Only three wooded lots left on the entire block now, I counted down. Soon birds, more adaptable than most other creatures, would be the only wild things left to share our neighborhood. Ah, well, so it goes. Humankind's dominance bulldozing along. City folk reaching out to vacation in suburbia, where they can watch the wild animals roam.

"I'll surround them with daisies when it warms a bit," I said as I looked at the crocuses in bloom.

I sat stroking Bundy and Sammie for a long while afterward. Their purrs were nice, but they would never ever be able to say a word to me. If Arnie could learn to talk, could another starling? Even if it couldn't, wouldn't it have the same basic personality? I'd never missed a creature so much in my life! The songs of the birds outside were cheering all of a sudden. Were they the songs of courtship already? Of the mating season? It was almost April. It wouldn't be long before the trees would be filled with the demanding chirps of newly hatched baby birds of all kinds.

Picking up the phone book, I looked up a very special number and punched it. "Hello. Audubon Society? Do people ever bring you orphaned starlings in the spring? I know where there's a wonderful home waiting if you should happen to get one and don't know what to do with it."

Who knows? There are many mysteries in the universe and undoubtedly more to the almighty plan than we mere mortals have yet discovered. Maybe there is a wheel of life included in that plan. Maybe there is such a thing as reincarnation, even for the simple, insignificant, wonderful little creatures that add so much wonder, so much joy to our world. Including starlings.

One way or another, I was certain that somewhere out in the world this coming May, there would be a lost, lonely, impertinent baby starling waiting to be rescued by someone who'd learned to appreciate the uniqueness of that species—someone like me. Perhaps someday there would be another Arnie for Margarete.

The publishers hope that this
Large Print Book has brought
you pleasurable reading.
Each title is designed to make
the text as easy to see as possible.
G. K. Hall Large Print Books
are available from your library and
your local bookstore. Or, you can
receive information by mail on
upcoming and current Large Print Books
and order directly from the publishers.
Just send your name and address to:

G. K. Hall & Co.
70 Lincoln Street
Boston, Mass. 02111

or call, toll-free:

1-800-343-2806

A note on the text
Large print edition designed by
Bernadette Montalvo.
Composed in 16 pt Plantin
on a Mergenthaler 202
by Compset Inc., Beverly MA.